Unlocking the Secrets of the
Gospel according to Thomas

Unlocking the Secrets of the *Gospel according to Thomas*

A Radical Faith for a New Age

CHARLES W. HEDRICK

CASCADE *Books* • Eugene, Oregon

UNLOCKING THE SECRETS OF THE *GOSPEL ACCORDING TO THOMAS*
A Radical Faith for a New Age

Copyright © 2010 Charles W. Hedrick. All rights reserved. Except for brief quotations in critical publications or reviews, no part of this book may be reproduced in any manner without prior written permission from the publisher. Write: Permissions, Wipf and Stock Publishers, 199 W. 8th Ave., Suite 3, Eugene, OR 97401.

Cascade Books
An Imprint of Wipf and Stock Publishers
199 W. 8th Ave., Suite 3
Eugene, OR 97401

www.wipfandstock.com

ISBN 13: 978-1-55635-239-3

Cataloging-in-Publication data:

Hedrick, Charles W.
    Unlocking the secrets of the gospel according to Thomas : a radical faith for a new age / Charles W. Hedrick.

    ISBN 13: 978-1-55635-239-3

    xvi + 230 p. ; 23 cm. — Includes bibliographical references, glossary, and indexes.

    1. Gospel of Thomas (Coptic Gospel)—Commentaries. 2. Gospel of Thomas (Coptic Gospel)—Criticism, interpretation, etc. I. Title.

BS2860 T52 H44 2010

Manufactured in the U.S.A.

*To the unnamed muse
who in every generation
has inspired courageous souls
with the spirit of criticism.*

I tell my secrets to those who [seek my] secrets.
Gospel of Thomas 62a

Contents

Preface ix
Abbreviations xiii

A Reader's Introduction 1

Translation and Commentary 19

Bibliography 189
Glossary 195
Index of Modern Authors 203
Index of Ancient Sources 205

Preface

The most famous manuscript discovery of the twentieth century for students of the Jesus tradition was the Coptic *Gospel according to Thomas*,[1] which was published in a modern language for the first time in 1959.[2] Since then *Thomas* has been translated into many different languages and numerous times into English. The English translations on the whole tend to be rather literal and hence wooden to the ear. My goal in this book is to produce a reader-friendly translation in contemporary idiomatic English. The resulting translation, while somewhat interpretive, is true to the Coptic—but every translation of any text from one language to another is interpretive. The present translation is supported by a commentary on each saying of Jesus. *Thomas* is a collection of sayings attributed to Jesus—simply sayings with no narrative literary context, or apparent order. The difference of this gospel from the canonical gospels is immediately evident: in the canonical gospels the sayings of Jesus are embedded in narrative with surrounding literary context. The evangelists have worked the sayings into their plots in different ways.

The editors of the first translation of *Thomas* counted 114 separate entries (they are unnumbered in the Coptic text). Most of the entries are simply sayings introduced by a brief "Jesus said" (86 in number). Four sayings are introduced by "he said" (sayings 1, 8, 65, and 74). There are two brief dialogues introduced by questions from the disciples (sayings 6 and 12) and a number of dialogues introduced by statements from the disciples as a group (sayings 18, 20, 24, 37, 43, 51, 52, 53, 99, and 113) or by others (either an anonymous "they" or a particular individual: sayings 21, 72, 79, 91, 104, and 114). Only two introductions deviate from

   1. The Coptic version of the *Gospel of Thomas* was discovered as part of the Nag Hammadi codices. A brief popular account can be found in Robinson, *The Nag Hammadi Library*, 22–26.
   2. Guillaumont et al., *The Gospel according to Thomas*.

these patterns (22, 100). In three cases the editors emended the text and began a new saying with "Jesus said," giving the emended saying a separate number (27, 93, 101). Once they emended the text and introduced a dialogue by "they said" (60). They divided what was apparently one saying introduced by "Jesus said" into two parts (69a and 69b) because they could easily tell that that the second saying was independent of the first, even if it was not introduced by an introductory statement of any sort. In another instance the editors divided an apparent dialogue into two separate sayings (74 and 75). Hence the present number of sayings in *Thomas* (114) is a scholarly convention decided by the first editors of the text, and raises the question how many of the numbered sayings may actually incorporate multiple independent sayings. In any case, it is unnecessary to repeat "Jesus said" before each saying in the translation, since it is clear from the narrative frame (the prologue) that each saying was attributed to Jesus. Thus I have eliminated the redundant usage of "Jesus said" or "he said" in this translation.

Most of the sayings of Jesus in *Thomas* have parallels in the canonical gospels; very few do not have such parallels. In many cases *Thomas* has introduced as a single saying a combination of two or more sayings appearing in the canonical gospels as independent sayings (for example, 16a and 16b), or has treated two sayings as one saying, one of which has a parallel in the canonical gospels and the other does not (for example, 4a and 4b). Often multiple sayings appear under one number but are easily recognizable as independent sayings (for example, saying 21). If a saying is recognizable as a distinctive and independent saying because it appears elsewhere as a saying unrelated to the sayings around it, it will be treated as an independent saying and given a separate number in this translation. The rationale for treating the material in this fashion is that it gives each saying its due recognition as an independent saying and at the same time preserves the association in which *Thomas* reports it. It is by no means certain, however, that the usual modern numbering system in *Thomas* reflects the philosophical sensitivities of a single ancient scribe.

This decision has necessitated dividing up *Thomas* sayings into "subsayings" so as to acknowledge the character of each as independent from the sayings around it. It has been necessary to do this a total of nineteen times (3, 4, 6, 11, 14, 16, 19, 21, 33, 39, 45, 47, 61, 62, 64, 69, 76, 77, 79). A similar situation exists in the canonical gospels, where sayings are not always reproduced in the same literary context in the different gospels (compare, for example, Matt 13:10–17; Mark 4:10–25; Luke 8:9–24). I have, however, retained the traditional numeration of the *Thomas* sayings (see the commentary), even when I divide sayings into subsayings.

Language, both written and spoken, remains a slippery means of communication, even though it is the only means of personal communication we have. We frequently misconstrue conversations in which we have taken part, or misinterpret written texts—and in regard to these spoken and written communications we have the advantage of a social and literary context to help us put things into perspective. In the case of narratives (like the canonical gospels, for example) statements included in the narrative derive their significance from the narrative context and the interpreter's own personal experience. For example, both Matthew and Luke reproduce a story about a lost sheep (Matt 18:12–13 = Luke 15:4–6) in different narrative contexts. In Matthew it appears in a chapter devoted to discipleship issues (the "little ones" of 18:6, 10). In this context the lost sheep takes on the character of a "disciple" and the story is about the disciples' preservation (18:14). Luke, however, tells the story in the context of Jesus's defense of his practice of accepting sinners (15:1–3a)—thus identifying the "sinner" as the lost sheep that was found (15:7). Matthew's story, on the one hand, is about the preservation of the righteous, and Luke's story, on the other, is about the saving of lost sinners.

In the case of *Thomas* no such narrative context exists. *Thomas* is not a narrative but a collection of sayings that can easily increase or decrease with no harm to the collection every time it was copied over its viable lifetime in antiquity (roughly 100–340 CE).[3] Each saying in *Thomas* therefore is subject to being read in a variety of social contexts over its viable life in the ancient world—and now also in the modern world, as well. Hence there is no one inevitable meaning to a given saying; in one sense there are as many meanings as there are readers willing to assign a meaning to a given saying. *Thomas* would have had a range of meanings for its ancient readers, where what it meant depended on how each reader read the saying. There is no one authoritative explanation for these sayings—nor was there ever!

---

3. For the date of the origin of the text see below; for the date of the manufacture of the Nag Hammadi codices, see Robinson, "Foreword," vii–x in Barnes, et al., *Cartonnage of the Covers*.

Abbreviations

AB	Anchor Bible
ABD	*Anchor Bible Dictionary*
Acts John	*Acts of John*
Acts Pet.	*Acts of Peter*
Acts Thom.	*Acts of Thomas*
Ant.	*Jewish Antiquities*
Alleg. Interp.	*Allegorical Interpretation*
Ap. John	*Apocryphon of John*
Apoc. Adam	*Apocalypse of Adam*
Apoc. Jas.	*Apocalypse of James*
Apoc. Mos.	*Apocalypse of Moses*
Apoc. Paul	*Apocalypse of Paul*
Apoc. Pet.	*Apocalypse of Peter*
Apol.	*Apology*
Auth. Teach.	*Authoritative Teaching*
Barn.	*Epistle of Barnabas*
Bek.	*Bekhorot*
Catech.	*Catechetical Lectures*
Catech. myst.	*Catechetical Lectures (On the Mysteries)*
Cels.	*Against Celsus*
c. h.	*Celestial Hierarchy*
Clem.	*Clement*
Cor	Corinthians
Corp. herm.	*Corpus hermeticum*
Col	Colossians
Cyr. H.	*Cyril of Jerusalem*
Dan	Daniel
Descr.	*Description of Greece*
Deut	Deuteronomy
Dial.	*Dialogue with Trypho*

Abbreviations

Dial. Sav.	*Dialogue of the Savior*
Did.	*Didache*
Didasc. Apost.	*Didascalia Apostolorum*
Diogn.	*Epistle to Diognetus*
Dion. Ar.	Pseudo-Dionysius Aeropagita
Disc.	*Discourse on the Eighth and Ninth*
Div.	*On Divination*
d. n.	*Divine Names* (Cicero)
e. h.	*Ecclesiastical Hierarchy*
Eccl	Ecclesiastes
Eccl. Hist.	*Ecclesiastical History*
En.	*Enoch*
Enn.	*Enneads*
ep.	*epistulae*
Ep. Apost.	*Epistula Apostolorum*
Eph	Ephesians
Epid.	*Epideixis (Demonstration of the Apostolic Preaching)*
Ep. Pet. Phil.	*Letter of Peter to Philip*
EPRO	Études preleminaires aux religions orientals dans l'empire romain
Esd.	Esdras
Eugnostos	*Eugnostos the Blessed*
Exc.	*Excerpts from Theodotus*
Exeg. Soul	*Exegesis on the Soul*
Exod	Exodus
Ezek	Ezekiel
Gal	Galatians
Gen	Genesis
Gos. Eb.	*Gospel of the Ebionites*
Gos. Eg.	*Gospel of the Egyptians*
Gos. Heb.	*Gospel of the Hebrews*
Gos. Judas	*Gospel of Judas*
Gos. Mary	*Gospel of Mary*
Gos. Pet.	*Gospel of Peter*
Gos. Phil.	*Gospel of Philip*
Gos. Sav.	*Gospel of the Savior*
Gos. Thom.	*Gospel of Thomas*
Gos. Truth	*Gospel of Truth*
Haer.	*Against Heresies*

Abbreviations

Heb	Hebrews
Herm. *Sim.*	Shepherd of Hermas, *Similitude*
Hom. Jer.	*Homiliae in Jeremiam*
Hom. Luc.	*Homiliae in Lucam*
Hos	Hosea
Hyp. Arch.	*Hypostasis of the Archons*
In Ph.	*In Aristotelis Physica commentaria*
Inst.	*The Divine Institutes*
Isa	Isaiah
J.W.	*Jewish War*
Jer	Jeremiah
Jas	James
Judg	Judges
Jdt	Judith
LCL	Loeb Classical Library
Leg.	*Contra adversarium legis et prophetarum*
Lev	Leviticus
LXX	Septuagint
Macc	Maccabees
Mal	Malachi
Math.	*Against the Mathematicians*
Matt	Matthew
Metaph.	*Metaphysics*
Mic	Micah
Mor.	*Moralia*
Mos.	*On the Life of Moses*
Myst.	*De mystica theologia*
Nat.	*Natural History*
NHC	Nag Hammadi Codex
NHS	Nag Hammadi Studies
NovT	*Novum Testamentum*
NT	New Testament
Num	Numbers
Orig. World	*On the Origin of the World*
Paed.	*Paedagogus (Christ the Educator)*
Pan.	*Panarion*
Paraph. Shem	*Paraphrase of Shem*
Parm.	*Parmenides*
1 Pet	1 Peter

Abbreviations

2 Pet	2 Peter
Phaed.	*Phaedo*
Phil	Philippians
Plant.	*De plantation*
Pol.	*To Polycarp*
P. Oxy.	Oxyrhynchus Papyrus
Princ.	*principiis* (First Principles)
Prov	Proverbs
PRSt	*Perspectives in Religious Studies*
Pr. Thanks.	*Prayer of Thanksgiving*
Ps	Psalms
Quis div.	*Quis dives salvetur* (Salvation of the Rich)
Ref.	*Refutation of All Heresies*
Resp.	*Respublica* (the Republic)
Recogn .	Pseudo-Clementine Recognitions
Rev	Revelation
Rom	Romans
Sam	Samuel
SBLTT	Society of Biblical Literature Texts and Translations
SecCent	*Second Century*
Sent. Sextus	*Sentences of Sextus*
Sir	Sirach
Strom.	*Stromata* (Miscellanies)
TDNT	*Theological Dictionary of the New Testament*
Teach. Silv.	*Teachings of Silvanus*
Test.	*To Quirinus: Testimonies against the Jews*
Test. Moses	*Testament of Moses*
Testim. Truth	*Testimony of Truth*
Thess	Thessalonians
Thom. Cont.	*Book of Thomas, the Contender*
Tim.	*Timaeus*
Tim	Timothy
Treat. Seth	*Second Treatise of the Great Seth*
Tri. Trac.	*Tripartite Tractate*
Vit. Plot.	*Vita Plotini*
Wis	Wisdom of Solomon
WUNT	Wissenschaftliche Untersuchungen zum Neuen Testamentum
Zech	Zechariah

A Reader's Introduction

GETTING STARTED

How old is the *Gospel of Thomas*?

The earliest mention of a *Gospel of Thomas* comes near the beginning of the third century. Origen, originally from Alexandria (died 253–254), quoted a saying, which appears as saying 82 of the version of the *Gospel of Thomas* we know today. Origen is unsure whether it is a genuine saying of Jesus (*Hom. Jer.* 20.3), and wasn't quite sure where he had read the saying. Considering his view of the *Gospel of Thomas* he knew (i.e., it was only an [human] "attempt" to write a gospel, whereas the canonical four were written by the Holy Spirit: *Hom. Luc.* 1, on Luke chapter 2), it is unlikely that he had read the saying in the version of *Thomas* we know today, which he surely would have rejected. Hence our *Gospel of Thomas* is not likely exactly the same one Origen knew. Hippolytus (died 235) mentions a *Gospel of Thomas* as one text from which the Naassenes (*Ref.* 5.7.20) were thought to derive their heretical teaching. The Naassene gospel has a brief saying that appears in neither today's (sayings) *Gospel of Thomas* nor the *Infancy Gospel of Thomas*. Later, in the first half of the fourth century, Eusebius mentions a *Gospel of Thomas* as one of those books "put forward by heretics under the names of apostles" (*Eccl. Hist.* 3.25.6). Hippolytus and Eusebius are part of what later in the fourth and fifth centuries dominated the early Christian movements, by calling themselves the "orthodox" (i.e., having the right belief). They rejected the version of the *Gospel of Thomas* known to them as spurious and untrustworthy. Another (second-century) writing bearing the title *Gospel of Thomas* modern scholars have dubbed the *Infancy Gospel of Thomas* (it has a series of stories describing the escapades of Jesus as a precocious child) to distinguish it from the (sayings) Gospel known today as the *Gospel of Thomas*.[1] Cyril of Jerusalem (died 386) warns against reading a Manichaean *Gospel of Thomas* written by a "wicked disciple" of Mani (*Catech.* 6:31; 4:36). The Stichometry of Nicephorus (bishop of Constantinople, 806–815) mentions a certain apocryphal *Gospel of Thomas* as having 1300 lines.[2] This survey of the secondary evidence of the period illustrates the difficulty of making a conclusive identification of our current (sayings) *Gospel of Thomas* with any of these texts mentioned in antiquity.[3] Hence none of these references helps in establishing an earliest possible date for the *Gospel of Thomas* known today as the (sayings) *Gospel of Thomas*.

An exciting discovery of three Greek fragments, described as vestiges of an "unknown gospel," however, occurred during a series of excavations from 1896 to 1907 at Oxyrhynchus in Egypt. One fragment, Oxyrhynchus Papyrus 1, described by its editors Bernard P. Grenfell and Arthur S. Hunt as a "collection of Sayings of our Lord," was published in 1897.[4] They dated the fragment on the basis of its handwriting as "not much later than the year 200"[5] but argued that it originated much earlier: "This Gospel, of which only a few extracts survive, was probably written about the beginning of the second century."[6] In a subsequent publication they held that the sayings "were earlier than 140 AD, and might go back to the first century."[7] When a second similar fragment surfaced among the papyri (P. Oxy. 654), they identified this second fragment as part of the same gospel as P. Oxy. 1, but it was obviously not the same exemplar, since P. Oxy. 1 was a leaf of a codex, and P. Oxy. 654 was part of a papyrus scroll.[8] The latest date for the composition of P. Oxy 654 they gave as 140.[9] A third fragment (P. Oxy. 655), which Grenfell and Hunt did not associate with P. Oxy. 1 and 654 (likely because P. Oxy 655 is written in a different

---

1. Hock, *Infancy Gospels of James and Thomas*, 83–146.
2. Schneemelcher and Wilson, *New Testament Apocrypha*, 1.41–42.
3. See Attridge, "Greek Fragments," 96–109 for the ancient literature on the *Gospel of Thomas*.
4. Grenfell and Hunt, *ΛΟΓΙΑ ΙΗΣΟΥ*, 5.
5. Ibid., 6.
6. Ibid., 16.
7. Grenfell and Hunt, *Oxyrhynchus Papyri Part 1*, 2.
8. Grenfell and Hunt, *Oxyrhynchus Papyri Part IV*, 10.
9. Ibid., 14–15.

hand than P. Oxy. 654), they dated as coming from a gospel that "is likely to have been composed in Egypt before A.D. 150."[10] The manuscript itself, however, they dated "as not likely to have been written later than A.D. 250."[11] Hence the three Greek fragments represent three different exemplars of an "unknown gospel."

In 1945 near Nag Hammadi in Upper Egypt, a virtually complete Coptic version of a (sayings) *Gospel of Thomas* was found among the texts of the Nag Hammadi Library. *Thomas* was the earliest of the fifty-two individual writings of the Library to be published (in 1959). This Coptic version has been dated to the fourth century, on the basis of the cartonnage included in the covers.[12] The three Greek fragments, discussed above, discovered at the end of the nineteenth century have been found to represent earlier Greek versions of the Coptic *Gospel of Thomas* known from the Nag Hammadi Library, although apparently none of them represent the particular text from which the Coptic version is a translation.[13] Hence, according to the current available evidence, the *Gospel of Thomas* was "composed," or better yet "compiled" for the first time by the late first or early second century (based on the Greek fragments), and perhaps earlier. The Greek fragments and the Coptic version together represent four different ancient published versions of the sayings *Gospel of Thomas*. The different versions attest to its popularity in the ancient world.

Where and by whom were the sayings first compiled?

No conclusive evidence exists to describe a particular geographical location for *Thomas*'s origin, and nothing is known of its compiler(s). The importance of the apostle Thomas to early Christianity in the East[14] has, however, led most scholars to posit the origin of the *Gospel of Thomas* in Syria, probably in the city of Edessa.[15] Christianity came to Edessa early,

---

10. Ibid., 28. See plates I and II at the end of the volume for photographs.
11. Ibid., 23.
12. Robinson, "Foreword," viii in Barnes, et al., *Cartonnage of the Covers*.
13. Attridge, "Greek Fragments," 96–102.
14. See the brief sketch of *Thomas* traditions by Drijvers, "Acts of Thomas," 324–25.
15. Koester, *Trajectories*, 126–29. *Thomas* appears only in the prologue and in saying 13, however. On the other hand, since the Apostle Thomas plays a significant role in John's Gospel (John 11 and 20), one might associate the origin of the *Gospel of Thomas*

and its character is shown by the evidence to be heterogeneous rather than orthodox—in other words, Christianity in Edessa in the early period is not consistent with later creedal Christianity.[16] According to Walter Bauer, Christianity first came to Edessa not much later than 150 in the form of Marcionism.[17]

On the other hand, it is entirely possible that the first compilation of the *Gospel of Thomas* was made in Egypt, although it may not initially have been associated with the Apostle Thomas. It is generally accepted, for example, that even the canonical gospels were originally anonymous, so it would be odd to argue that the Apostle Thomas was its original compiler, or that the name of the Apostle Thomas was part of the original subtitle or prologue.[18] It is generally recognized that at some point a compiler chose "a disciple of Jesus as guarantor for its message,"[19] and attributed the text to Thomas since he was one of the apostles named in the text (James is mentioned in saying 12, and Peter, Matthew, and Thomas in saying 13). In the canonical gospels, the name of Matthew appears in the gospel that traditionally bears his name (Matt 9:9; 10:3). The names of the evangelists Mark, Luke, and John do not appear in the gospels bearing their names. Those few sayings that may reflect a Syriac influence could easily have been added to the collection at some later date, and the text associated with the apostle Thomas when the text was appropriated for use by Syrian Christians.[20]

The only unambiguous and concrete connection the *Gospel of Thomas* has with any particular geographical location is to Upper Egypt—all extant manuscripts were discovered either at Oxyrhynchus or near the large city of Nag Hammadi.[21] Christianity first came to Egypt at the beginning

---

with Ephesus in Asia Minor, where John's gospel may have originated; see Brown, *Gospel according to John*, 1:ciii–civ. This idea was suggested to me by Douglas Parrott.

16. Bauer, *Orthodoxy and Heresy*, 1–43.

17. Ibid., 29, 43.

18. See, for example, Perrin, *Introduction to the New Testament*, 163, 169, 222; and Marxsen, *Introduction to the New Testament*, 142, 152, 161, 259.

19. Plisch, *Thomas*, 17.

20. See Guillaumont, "Sémitismes." See Helmut Koester on Syrian traditions in Egypt, *Introduction*, 2:228–29. If missionaries from Palestine and Syria brought Christianity to Egypt, they also opened a way for influence to flow the other way as well.

21. Of course, Egypt was one of the few places in the world where the climate allowed ancient manuscripts to survive; but that datum should not be used to dismiss the fact

of the second century CE and was of a Gentile "syncretistic-gnostic" type, a suitable matrix for the compiling of a list of Jesus sayings, such as appears in the *Gospel of Thomas*.[22]

Judaism, however, had been in Egypt since the sixth century BCE, and there were substantial Jewish communities at Alexandria, Leontopolis, Oxyrhynchus, and Apollonopolis Magna (modern Edfu). There were even two Jewish temples erected in Egypt, one at Elephantine and another at Leontopolis. By the early first century CE it has been estimated that the Jewish population in Egypt "numbered in the hundreds of thousands."[23] From the evidence, Judaism in Egypt reflects a significant influence by Graeco-Roman traditions. Relations with the Roman authorities were generally quite good, and the Jews enjoyed the right to worship and live their lives as they chose with little interference. The generally peaceful coexistence of Jews and Greeks in Egypt was marred by a massacre (pogrom) of Jews by the Greek citizens of the city of Alexandria in 38 CE. In 115 Egyptian Jews revolted against Rome, and the response from the authorities was so devastating that the Jewish community never recovered.

The Jews in Egypt, however, did not join the Jewish revolt of 66–70 in Judea that resulted in the destruction of Jerusalem and the Jewish temple. As a consequence, Egypt would have seemed to Jews in Palestine as an attractive place of refuge, particularly in the pre-70 period, before the Roman destruction of Jerusalem.[24] It would be surprising to learn that no followers of Jesus had been among those "Jews" migrating to Egypt before the war or taken there in slavery after the war.[25]

---

that Egypt (Alexandria) is as plausible a place of origin for the *Gospel of Thomas* as Syria (Edessa)—and perhaps better.

22. Bauer, *Orthodoxy and Heresy*, 53.

23. Pearson, "Alexandria," 153.

24. Eusebius reports that the members of the church at Jerusalem received an oracle to go to Pella, a Greek city of the Decapolis, to which they fled before the war with Rome (*Eccl. Hist.*, 3.5). Earlier persecutions against the followers of Jesus resulted in many of them leaving the city: and they went "on their way to all the heathen" (Eusebius *Eccl. Hist.* 3.2; Acts 8:1–5; 11:19–20; 12:1–5). Acts 2:10 suggests the ease of interaction between Jerusalem and Egypt.

25. Bell, *Cults and Creeds*, 25–49; Lewis, *Life in Egypt*, 28–31; Pearson; "Alexandria," 153; and Smallwood, *Jews under Roman Rule*, 220–55, 389–427.

Unlocking the Secrets of the *Gospel according to Thomas*

GETTING ORIENTED

What are some distinctive literary features of the *Gospel of Thomas*?

A variety of literary forms are represented in the collection—for example parables (saying 63), macarisms (sayings 69a and 69b), woes (saying 112), prophetic sayings (saying 82), community rules (saying 6), proverbs/aphorisms (saying 47b), dialogues (saying 13), and *chreiae*/pronouncement stories (saying 91). In other words, *Thomas* is clearly eclectic, not only in the logic of its sayings but also in the oral/literary forms of the tradition it uses. Most of *Thomas*'s sayings are shared with sayings of Jesus found in the Synoptic Gospels (for example, sayings 9, 26, 31, 32, 86, and 100), or are variations of sayings known in the Synoptic Gospels (for example, saying 36 // Luke 12:22), but there are also sayings attributed to Jesus obviously not originating with him (for example, see sayings 102 and 8 for fables of Aesop, and for Jewish wisdom literature, see saying 17). One striking feature is that *Thomas* does not quote the Hebrew Bible (the Old Testament) as a source of authority but introduces as sayings of Jesus material known from the Hebrew Bible (saying 16b). It is not clear whether *Thomas* is even aware of the Hebrew Bible; it is clear that if *Thomas* knows the Hebrew Bible, it is not an authoritative text for whoever compiled the collection. In some cases *Thomas* attributes sayings to Jesus that would fit with the material selected by the canonical evangelists had they but known them (for example, sayings 39a and 82).

The *Gospel of Thomas* represents a selection of material made at different times by different collectors over at least 240 years (from the second century to the middle of the fourth century) in at least two languages (Greek and Coptic).[26] Under such conditions a deliberate plan for the order of the sayings in *Thomas*, if there ever was one, would be virtually impossible to detect. Not surprisingly, scholars have been unable to agree on a logical order for the sayings. While the use of "catchwords" as mnemonic devices seems clear in some cases (for example, the word "cast" [ⲛⲟⲩϫⲉ] in sayings 8–10 or the theme of coming [ⲉⲓ and ⲛⲏⲩ] in the series of sayings in 21). Some sayings may have been grouped on the basis

---

26. Guillaumont, "Sémitismes." Guillaumont argues for an Aramaic and Syriac stage to *Thomas* on the basis of certain sayings in *Thomas*.

of similar ideas (the motifs of seeking, finding, and knowing in sayings 1–6). In other cases it seems obvious that sayings are grouped on the basis of literary form (sayings 63–65, 97–98). Perhaps in some cases, it may even be possible to find an interpretive arrangement of certain sayings (for example, sayings 32, 33a, and 33b; 65 and 66; 73–75). Nevertheless, such groupings have not been helpful in determining a rationale for the arrangement of the sayings in *Thomas* as a whole.

Where they overlap, the Greek fragments are not always consistent with the Coptic exemplar, and this leads to the conclusion that the Greek fragments do not represent the Greek text from which the Coptic was a translation. The Greek and Coptic texts overlap in the following material and in the following way:

- P. Oxy. 1 = Coptic sayings 26–29 and 30 (+77b), 31–33;
- P. Oxy. 654 = Coptic sayings prologue and sayings 1–7;
- P. Oxy. 655 = Coptic sayings 24, 36–39.

For examples of the imprecise parallels between the Greek and the Coptic in some of the sayings, see 2, 3, 5, 30 (+77b).

The theory that the *Gospel of Thomas* is a collection of collections having the innate potential of being "adjusted" (i.e., sayings added, deleted, or further modified in some way) every time a new copy is produced or translated into a new language is in part supported by the duplicates of sayings (3a and 113; 5 and 6b; 48 and 106; 55 and 101; 56, 80, and 111; 87 and 112) and striking contradictions (95 and 109 [lending money]). Such features are more easily explained as scribal oversights than as a deliberate editorial strategy. A similar use of duplicated material appears in the canonical gospels as well (for example, Matt 12:38–39 and Matt 16:1–4; Matt 5:31–32 and Matt 19:9).

Does the *Gospel of Thomas* have a consistent theology?

It is not possible to describe a consistent systematic theology for the *Gospel of Thomas* because its diverse collection of sayings does not represent a composition by a single author or even the ideas of a single speaker. Each saying was gathered on the basis of how it was understood (i.e., interpreted) by a scribal collector, and how the scribe may have understood the saying does not necessarily fit the obvious logic of the saying. See, for example, Luke's reading (18:1, 6–8) of Jesus's story (18:2–5) of the judge and the widow; only in Luke's mind does the story relate to persistence in prayer and the return of the Lord.[27] Only a small percentage of the sayings actually originated with the historical man Jesus of Nazareth, while the rest of the sayings originated at different times in diverse and unknown locations and represent the work of Jesus's followers, who attributed ideas to him.[28] It is possible, however, to describe a spectrum of related religious ideas and patterns emerging in the sayings (see the discussion below).

The lack of a narrative context for the sayings and the uncertainty of a known social context for the text as a whole present a difficult problem to translators, interpreters, and readers. I have aimed at explaining the Coptic text (not the Greek fragments) as they might have been understood in the geographical context of the Coptic language, that is, in the social context of Egypt and Ethiopia in the second century and later. Or put another way, the sayings in the collection no longer derive (if they ever did) from a Jewish teacher in rural Galilee in the first third of the first century, but they have become sayings of a bearer of divine revelation, a mystagogue, likely in the cosmopolitan city of Alexandria, but certainly somewhere in Egypt. Given this situation, many (if not most) of the sayings are obscure (for example, see the commentary to sayings 10, 40, 41, 87, 88, and 105), particularly in light of the fact that the initial frame to the text (prologue and saying 1) affirms that no matter how plain or obvious the logic of a saying may appear, there are hidden meanings that must be intuited.

Even if a social context were known, statements lacking a narrative context can still be read in a surprising number of ways. Here are two examples. Mark 4:24 in its literary context (Mark 4:10–25) relates to the parables Jesus speaks. Those about him with the Twelve have been made privy to the secret of the imperial rule of God (Mark 4:11); everyone else, however, hears only the story, but is not privy to the secret of the imperial rule (Mark 4:10–12). Jesus then tells them when they are alone (Mark 4:10) the interpretation of the parable of the sower (Mark 4:13–20). On the basis of Mark's narrative context, this particular interpretation of the parable should have been obvious to them (Mark 4:21–23). In this context Mark 4:24 seems to have the weight of, "listen carefully to what you hear,

27. Hedrick, *Parables as Poetic Fictions*, 187–207.
28. Funk et al., *Five Gospels*, 471–532.

for your evaluation of what you hear will determine what you get from the parable." Others not privy to the secret of the imperial rule will lose even the little understanding they may have (Mark 4:25). On the other hand, the same saying is reproduced by Matthew and Luke, where it has to do with the judging and forgiving of others. In Matt 7:2 the saying is in parallelism with the idea that you will be judged with the same judgment you give to others. In Luke 6:37–38 the saying affirms that you will receive forgiveness as you forgive others. In this way, contexts both social and literary slant how statements are understood.

Here is another example, with a saying that appears in Matthew and Luke and the *Gospel of Thomas* (saying 34). The saying about a blind person leading a blind person and both falling into a ditch (Luke 6:39) is odd. A natural question about this curious situation is, why would a blind person undertake to lead another blind person anyway? In such a circumstance it is not surprising that both would fall into a ditch. Luke's explanation (Luke 6:40) of the aphorism applies it to disciples and teachers: disciples are not greater than their teachers, but when fully taught they become like the teacher (a case of the blind leading the blind). The aphorism also appears in Matt 15:14, where it is treated as unambiguous and self-evident discourse describing the Pharisees—not odd at all. They are blind guides leading the blind (15:12–14). Used in this way, the saying becomes satire, graphically caricaturing the Pharisees as religiously ignorant teachers who lead others who foolishly trust their guidance into a similar ignorance. The real aphorism in Matt 15:10–16, according to Matthew, on the other hand, is the saying about what goes into one's mouth not causing defilement; rather what defiles is what comes out of the mouth (15:11; compare Mark 7:14–15 and *Thomas* 14c). Matthew provides what seems to be an unnecessary explanation for the rather obvious saying (15:15–20; compare Mark 7:17–23). See the discussion of *Thomas* saying 34 in the following commentary.

It has always been the case that we readers participate in "making our own meaning" out of all our communication, written as well as spoken. This observation is as true of the biblical texts as it is of the sayings in the *Gospel of Thomas*. Writers produce texts in a particular language world at a particular historical moment. Such texts are weighted with particular cultural values. Readers engage these texts from the perspective of their own different life experiences and cultural values. Meanings are made by the reader in the nexus between the reader's world and the world of the text.[29] In short, texts do not have innate meanings; basically, at first glance, they are only squiggles on a page. The reader, if able competently to read the language in which the text is written and if gracious, confers meaning on the text—which may differ from the "meanings" made by other readers. This observation is nowhere more true than with the *Gospel of Thomas*, which contains sayings from different parts of the ancient world, dating over a three-hundred-year period.

A good example of this clash of worlds in the making of meaning is found in the way the early Christian writer Paul (Gal 3:6) reads an ancient Hebrew text (Gen 15:6) in its Greek translation, and the different reading of that same text by another early Christian writer, James (2:23). Paul argues that Abraham was declared righteous by God only through faith because Abraham lived before the law was given. Hence he concludes that obedience to the law cannot affect one's righteousness before God (Gal 2:15–16; 3:6–9). James, on the other hand, reads Gen 15:6 in the context of Abraham's sacrifice of Isaac (Gen 22:1–14) and argues that Abraham was declared righteous by both faith and works (Jas 2:21–24), for "faith without works is dead" (Jas 2:17). Modern readers (heirs of sixteenth-century Reformation Christianity) usually resolve this dilemma by opting for Paul's solution on the basis of what they bring to the text.

What are some distinctive religious ideas of the *Gospel of Thomas*?

Many sayings in *Thomas* reflect a radicalizing of the spiritual mysticism found in some of the earliest texts produced by the followers of Jesus. Mysticism as used with reference to *Thomas* "connotes a breaking down of all barriers in the immediacy of Divine Presence . . . and an assumed ontological merging of the finite with the Infinite."[30] For example, in *Thomas* the Divine is described as the One-Who-Lives: and whoever "lives out of the One-Who-Lives will never see death" (saying 111). One finds God by looking within and becoming one with the One (3a, 3b, 108, 11c, 18, 42).

---

29. Hedrick, *Many Things in Parables*, 46–54.
30. Harkness, *Mysticism*, 22.

Jesus is the living Jesus because he is the son of the One-who-Lives (prologue, 37, 59). Jesus is from the Equality, who brings forth the things of the Father (61b). He is from the Self-Originated Light; he is the light above everything, and is everything (saying 77a). His family, the children of the Light, comprise those who do the will of the Father (saying 99). His task is to speak sayings containing a secret meaning, which produces immortality in those who discover their interpretation (prologue). The message is unique (saying 17). He casts fire on the world and guards it (saying 10) and throws division into the world (16a, but cf. 72). He tells his mysteries to those who seek them (saying 62a, but cf. 92). Everything originally issued from him and will return to him (sayings 77a and 77b). His yoke is easy and his lordship is gentle, eventually bringing repose (saying 90). Union with him brings the revelation of the hidden things (saying 108). He makes women male so that they may become live spirits (114). In *Thomas* the status of Jesus encroaches on the role of the Father (saying 77a and 77b), not unlike in some passages in the New Testament (for example, Col 1:15–20).

The "world" represents an ethical construct diametrically opposed to the imperial rule of God (saying 21c). Hence followers of Jesus are to disengage completely from the structures of society (sayings 95, 64a and 64b). The imperial rule of God is a spiritual reality diametrically opposed to the "world" (saying 22), as such it is both an existential and social reality (saying 113), rather than otherworldly (sayings 51 and 11a). The ultimate destination of the follower of Jesus is not the Christian heaven or the new heavens and new earth of Jewish apocalyptic expectations (saying 51), but a spiritual journey into the One (sayings 49, 22, and 18).

Sayings in *Thomas* that reflect the greatest dependence on Graeco-Roman philosophical and religious ideas are 3b, 15, 17, 18, 19a, 21a, 22, 28, 42, 50, 61b, 75, 77a, 77b, 83, 84, 104, and 114. In terms of the schools of thought that seem the most influential are the diverse world of early Christianities, Platonism, and Hermeticism.

Did the *Gospel of Thomas* address a particular community?

Certain sayings seem to assume a user community (sayings 25, 26, 39a, 40, and 99), but generally *Thomas* reflects a universalism inviting anyone to share in its religious views by discovering the right interpretation of the words of Jesus (saying 1); thus the insider "community" is not closed, but always open. The opponents evoked in sayings 39a and 102 may well be representatives of Judaism or of those who call themselves "the Orthodox," that is, the early Catholic Church (cf. saying 44), which had been in Egypt by the beginning of the second century.[31] One finds a rejection or marginalizing of the authority invested in religious leaders (sayings 3a and 12). The usual markers of religious ritual in the ancient world (prayer, fasting, alms, diet [sayings 6, 14a, and 104]) are specifically rejected, although there are two sayings reflecting a concern for disinterested charity and concern for others (sayings 6a and 69b). The community seems to be comprised partly of neophytes, called disciples, who always ask the wrong questions, or who think at a natural level while Jesus is thinking on a deeper, spiritual plane (saying 22). On the other hand, only the advanced, described as the solitary and elect (sayings 16b and 49), will find the imperial rule—apparently because only they "found" the hidden interpretations of the sayings and achieved union with the One (saying 49). Three terms are apparently used to classify people. Those outside the community, involved in the structures of society (i.e., the world), are designated as "humanity's children" (saying 28). These people constitute everyone outside the community, still involved in the structures of society (i.e., the world). They are conceived as descendents of the first human being (Adam) after Adam's separation into male and female genders. "Adam's children" (saying 106), "children of the Light" (saying 50), or "children of the living Father" (saying 3b), on the other hand, are generic terms used for the members of the community. Mythically they are conceived as descendents of the first human being (Adam) while he was still an androgynous (male-female) whole, i.e., a singularity (sayings 86 and 106).

Beyond those sayings in *Thomas* that seem to suppose a community, we have no concrete evidence that a *Thomas* community ever actually existed. There is no archaeological evidence and no ancient site that can be connected to a group that can be associated with *Thomas*. There is, however, evidence that in early Hellenistic Christianity a group with similar esoteric proclivities existed in Paul's Corinthian community.[32] There are several overlaps between the interests of the Corinthian "spiritual"

---

31. Bauer, *Orthodoxy and Heresy*, 53.
32. Koester, *Ancient Christian Gospels*, 55–62; and Koester, *Introduction*, 2:120–26.

Christians" (1 Cor 3:1) and the *Gospel of Thomas*. Paul apparently picked up and used the terminology of that group in 1 Cor 2:7 (and elsewhere) and described himself as teaching at Corinth "a secret and hidden wisdom of God decreed before the ages." The idea reflected in the statement of "what is hidden being revealed" (cf. Mark 4:2) is a recurring theme in *Thomas* (sayings 5 and 6). Paul also quotes in this context a saying (1 Cor 2:9) that turns up in *Gos. Thom.* 17: "What no eye has seen, nor ear heard, nor the heart of man conceived, what God has prepared for those who love him." If we read Paul's irony about these spiritual Christians as language they used to describe themselves (1 Cor 4:8), they apparently conceived of themselves as "having become kings and reigning," concepts that also suit the interests of the *Thomas* community (sayings 2, 81, and 110). Such similarity of interest shows that esoteric ideas have been a part of Hellenistic Christianity since the earliest period. And that is clearly the case particularly with regard to Egypt, where the earliest forms of Christianity in the late first and early second centuries were esoteric and speculative.[33]

Are there typical Christian ideas that do not appear in the *Gospel of Thomas*?

Because of the emphasis they receive in the earliest writings of the Christian movements (for example, in the Pauline correspondence), one might expect to find sayings reflecting a crucifixion theology or an emphasis on the resurrection of Jesus in *Thomas*, but these do not appear. The cross appears in one saying (55) but is only used as an example of single-minded devotion. Instead of resurrection, *Thomas* emphasizes rest or repose (50, 51, 60, 86, 90). The term "living," rather than an allusion to the resurrection of Jesus, most likely is applied to Jesus (prologue, 37) because he is the son of the living Father/One (sayings 3b and 59). Note the epithet "the living one" for Jesus in Rev 1:18 and the use of "the living God" in the Hebrew Bible (e.g., Ps 42:2; 84:2; Isa 37:4, 17; Jer 10:10). Evil spirits and a personified evil (i.e., Satan) are not to be found, even though they are in the texts adopted by the framers of the creeds and canon. But the community appears to experience charismatically certain magical or mystical powers (19b, 106).

33. Koester, *Introduction*, 2:225–33.

Unlocking the Secrets of the *Gospel according to Thomas*

What surprising new ideas does the *Gospel of Thomas* offer not in other Christian texts?

"Salvation" is not a term used by *Thomas*, but the concept of the blessed state of the solitary is expressed in other ways. *Thomas* appropriates the term "imperial rule" (i.e., "kingdom"), a term known in Jewish apocalyptic and New Testament texts as a future otherworldly state—a place literally out of this world. In *Thomas* the futuristic expectation of the coming rule of God becomes a present existential experience (saying 113). *Thomas* employs different expressions for experiencing the imperial rule: one enters (saying 22), finds (saying 27), knows (saying 46), possesses (saying 54); or one is far from the imperial rule (saying 82). A similar lack of precision in describing the imperial rule is also found in the Synoptic Gospels (for example, in Mark 1:15; 9:1, 47; 10:15; 12:34). Another idea drawn from Hellenistic and Jewish tradition—the concept of rest or repose—is used in *Thomas* to describe the ultimate destination of the blessed soul (50, 51). Perhaps the most unusual idea *Thomas* uses is the concept of regaining Eden and the perfect state of the original human being before the fall (saying 18). Adam was created as a perfect androgynous whole, a male-female singularity (sayings 11c, 22, 29, and 85). But since Adam even in his singularity was conceived as "male" (but having both male and female principles), females must therefore become "male," in the unified sense that Adam was male (saying 114). In *Thomas* the union of male and female into a singularity was a mythical concept rather than a social concept like Paul's idea of unity or oneness for Jew and Greek, slave and free, male and female (Gal 3:28).

How is the *Gospel of Thomas* similar to and different from the Synoptic Gospels?

The commentary calls attention to the extensive amount of material *Thomas* shares with the Synoptic Gospels (Matthew, Mark, and Luke). *Thomas* reports the sayings it shares with the Synoptic Gospels with a degree of similarity and difference like the Synoptic Gospels themselves. Although scholars generally agree about the reasons for similarity and difference between the Synoptic Gospels, scholars have not been able to agree on the reasons for similarity and difference between *Thomas* and the Synoptic Gospels. Here is the issue into which the discussion has polarized: Is *Thomas* literarily dependent on the Synoptic Gospels, or does it draw from an independent oral tradition—at least in part?

Most scholars have come to the conclusion that the similarity and difference between the Synoptic Gospels is due to a number of factors: their common use of oral tradition, an independent literary dependence on Mark by Matthew and Luke, and the common and independent use by Matthew and Luke of a hypothetical source dubbed Q (*Quelle*, a German word meaning "source"). The explanation of the similarity and difference is referred to as the solution to the Synoptic Problem, and the problem simply stated is this: How does one explain the similarity and difference between the Synoptic Gospels?[34] Nevertheless, scholars have reached an impasse on the question of *Thomas*'s relationship to the Synoptic Gospels. The primary options for explaining their relationship are generally reduced to two: *Thomas* is independent of the Synoptic Gospels; *Thomas* is literarily dependent on the Synoptic Gospels. Those who find *Thomas* literarily dependent on the Synoptic Gospels simply dismiss the text as a late product having nothing to tell the scholar about early Jesus traditions.[35] Others, however, employ selected sayings in *Thomas* as significant witnesses in the study of the Jesus traditions.[36]

My own position with regard to *Thomas* and the Synoptic Gospels is this: *Thomas* represents a collection of collections.[37] Each saying must be individually considered and regarded as potentially independent until it can be shown to be dependent on the Synoptic Gospels.[38] This position has the effect of bringing the *Gospel of Thomas* into a discussion of the Synoptic Problem; so if for nothing else, the *Thomas* sayings can be used to critique the synoptic sayings, as scholars do now with the differences between Matthew, Mark, and Luke. Nevertheless, I have aimed at using neutral language in the commentary when discussing the parallels; I describe their similar traditions as shared, and allow synoptic sayings to

---

34. Hedrick, *When History and Faith Collide*, 76–109.
35. Meier, *A Marginal Jew*, 127.
36. Funk et al., *Five Gospels*, 471–532.
37. For a brief summary of positions taken with regard to the dependence/independence of the *Gospel of Thomas*, see Hedrick, "Anecdotal Argument," 114–15.
38. Hedrick, *Parables as Poetic Fictions*, 236–51.

play off *Thomas* sayings and vice versa in order to clarify the distinctive features of each saying.

Is the *Gospel of Thomas* a Gnostic text?

Thomas as a whole is not a Gnostic text, but it appears to represent a radicalizing of the early Jesus traditions—much if not most of its material derives from the earliest period of the Jesus movements (see the commentary for parallels to individual sayings). But it is also an eclectic text, and throughout its viable life it continued to draw on extraneous traditions in the Hellenistic world that suited its radicalizing and esoteric spirit (for example, 84). Although it does contain sayings that would be fully consonant with Gnostic ideas (for example, 7, 29, 114), it also contains sayings that are fully consonant with early Christianity (77b, 97, 98). Most commentaries finding *Thomas* to be thoroughly Gnostic find it to be so by interpreting the sayings against an assumed Gnostic background.[39] *Thomas* represents a stage in the trajectory of the Jesus traditions that falls somewhere between Paul, who used language and concepts that later came to characterize the developed Gnostic systems of the second century,[40] and the Gospel of John, which also uses language and concepts sympathetic to Gnosticism.[41] Neither Paul nor John is generally thought to be Gnostic, however. Nevertheless each writer shares in the thought-world that eventually produced what is known as Christian Gnosticism. *Thomas*, although roughly contemporary with the Gospel of John, is more closely aligned with the language-world of the early Jesus traditions than is John; *Thomas* is not a speculative treatise (like the Nag Hammadi writings the *Gospel of Truth* or the *Treatise on the Resurrection*) but primarily a repeating of the presumed founder's words. John, on the other hand, has moved considerably beyond the Jewish sayings tradition into a theological rewriting of the Jesus tradition that is considerably closer to

---

39. See, for example, the interpretation of saying 21 in Gärtner, *Theology*, 178–81.

40. Wilson, *Gnosis and the New Testament*, 49–55.

41. For Johannine features sympathetic to Gnosticism, see: Janssens, "Trimorphic Protennoia," 235–43; Dodd, *Fourth Gospel*, 97–114; and Koester, *Introduction*, 2:194–99.

Hellenistic thought[42]—although, to be sure, *Thomas* has also been influenced by Hellenistic thought (for example, sayings 3b, 49, 50, 61b).

How does the *Gospel of Thomas* relate to the historical Jesus?

The term *historical Jesus* simply means what can be known of the circumstances of the life of the Jewish man, Jesus of Nazareth, through modern historical-critical study of the sources without recourse to the inferences made by his early and later followers. In this regard the *Gospel of Thomas* is of no help, since the collectors of *Thomas* had no interest in the details of Jesus's personal life. It is not unreasonable to suppose, however, that some of the *Thomas* sayings might represent an early tradition independent of the canonical gospels, and some may even go back to the historical Jesus. Indeed, there are a number of the new sayings in *Thomas* that have been found to be compatible with those sayings reported in the canonical gospels.[43]

The oral Jesus tradition continued well into the second century, so there is no reason in principle why *Thomas* could not have had access to it as well as did the canonical evangelists and the other gospels known in the first and second centuries.[44] Even sayings in the canonical gospels must be analyzed to determine which sayings most probably originated with the historical Jesus. Here is one saying that likely Jesus did not originate, even though three of the canonical evangelists think he did (Mark 14:7; Matt 26:11; John 12:8), since it appears in Deut 15:11. So the best one could argue is that Jesus repeated it, but clearly did not originate it. As much as one might wish it otherwise, most things in the canonical gospels had a source other than Jesus.[45] And as surprising as it may seem to some, some noncanonical gospels do preserve sayings that originated with Jesus. For example, good cases can be made for two *Thomas* sayings, 82[46] and 98,[47] originating with Jesus of Nazareth.

---

42. Dodd, *Fourth Gospel*, 10–73.
43. Higgins, "Non-Gnostic Sayings," 295–301.
44. Hedrick, "34 Gospels."
45. See the rationales in the report of the Jesus Seminar: Funk et al., *Five Gospels*.
46. Hedrick, "An Anecdotal Argument," 119–24.
47. Hedrick, "Flawed Heroes."

Translation and Commentary

PROLOGUE

These secret sayings were spoken by the living Jesus and they were inscribed by his twin, Judas Thomas.

COMMENT

The prologue describes the sayings as secret or hidden, which means they are unknown to the public at large; but since many of the sayings are already known in early Christian literature, what is secret about them must be how they are understood in this text (see saying 1). The secrecy motif is widespread in antiquity, including both Christian (e.g., Mark 4:11 = Matt 13:11 = Luke 8:10; Rev 1:1–3; Rom 11:25–29) and Jewish (e.g., Dan 2:22, 30; 2 Esd 12:3–39; 14:1–5; *1 En.* 37–71) texts.

Jesus is called "the living Jesus" because he is the son of the "One-Who-Lives" (sayings 37, 111), who is also the "living Father" (sayings 3b and 50, and John 6:57). In sayings 77a, 77b, and 59 the living Jesus makes claims that presume on the divine prerogative. The designation *living Jesus* also appears in the *Apoc. Pet.* 81:17–18, where the living Jesus is actually an incorporeal figure, the intellectual Spirit filled with radiant light (83:1–15), and in Rev 1:18 where the resurrected Jesus is called "the living one." The tradition that Jesus had a twin brother is known in *Thom. Cont.* 138:1–12 (for the role of Thomas in this gospel, see saying 13). The appellation "living Jesus" may refer to the resurrected Jesus, who in the canonical tradition was present between his resurrection and ascension for some days (for example, Acts 1:3; 10:40–41; 13:30–31); see saying 38 about the absence of Jesus. The Greek parallel (Layton, *Nag Hammadi*, 113, 126) is very similar to the Coptic.

SAYING 1

Whoever discovers the explanation of these sayings will never die.

COMMENT

These sayings conceal secrets the knowledge of which brings immortality. Hence saying 1 sets the hermeneutical principle for understanding every saying in the collection. Each saying conceals a particular secret "meaning," which is the real subject of all the sayings. Their surface explanations are not at issue; rather the hidden, secret meaning is what is at stake. Whoever discovers the secret meaning of all sayings will never die (literally: "not taste death"); compare similar sayings in John (5:24; 8:51; 11:25–26). Thus potentially several levels of meaning exist in each saying: how the narrator of the prologue and saying 1 understands the sayings, the surface meaning of the words of each saying, and the multiple meaning(s) each reader thinks is the secret meaning. Paul describes a hidden secret "wisdom" possessed by those "who love God" (1 Cor 2:6–9). The *pesherim* at Qumran (e.g., the commentaries on Isaiah and Habakkuk) and Christian interpretations of Jesus's Jewish parables (e.g., Luke 18:1–8) are similar examples of finding new meanings in ancient texts. The Greek fragment of Coptic saying 1 (Layton, *Nag Hammadi*, 113, 126) is very similar to the Coptic.

SAYING 2

Seekers should not abandon their search before they make an unsettling discovery completely amazing them. They will then become rulers over everything.

COMMENT

Here is another saying stressing the search for the hidden meaning. Readers are encouraged to persevere. What they will discover if they do is not common wisdom but a shocking knowledge giving them authority to rule over all things. Becoming kings and rulers is a concept shared by the spiritual Christians at Corinth (1 Cor 4:8). Elsewhere in the New Testament the concept is met as "reigning with Christ" (Rom 5:17; 2 Tim 2:12; Rev 20:4, 6). Similar sayings are known in the *Gos. Heb.* (Clement of Alexandria, *Strom.*, 2.9.45 and 5.14.96: Miller, *Complete Gospels*, fragments 6a and 6b); in each of these citations "rest" is added as the final state, as also the Greek fragment of this saying has it (Layton, *Nag Hammadi*, 113, 126). In Coptic *Thomas*, however, the final state in this saying is to become a ruler over everything.

Unlocking the Secrets of the *Gospel according to Thomas*

SAYING 3A

If your leaders tell you the imperial rule is up there in the heavens, then the birds will get there first. If they say "in the sea," then the fish will beat you there. But God's imperial rule is inside you and all around you.

COMMENT

The translation "imperial rule of God" rather than the more usual "kingdom of God" emphasizes the exercise of God's authority that knows no borders. This saying of Jesus is also found in Luke 17:20–21, where it locates God's rule in your midst or within you (translations of the passage in Luke vary). But *Thomas* makes it quite clear that the imperial rule of God is both within you and all around you (see saying 113). The first half of the saying parodies God's rule as a location or place. Compare the *Teachings of Silvanus*: God "is the one who dwells in everyplace and also in no place" (116:19—117:5). God's imperial rule, however, is an inner spiritual experience ("inside you"), shared with others of like mind ("all around you"). See sayings 20, 51, and 113. The Greek fragment of 3a and 3b is slightly different (Layton, *Nag Hammadi* 114, 126). See the list of parallels to the idea of the internal/external character of the imperial rule in DeConick, *Original Gospel of Thomas*, 53.

SAYING 3B

If you know yourselves,
   then you will be known.
Only by knowing yourself
   will you recognize that you are children of the living Father.
If you do not know yourselves,
   you dwell in poverty and are completely impoverished.

COMMENT

The opening statement ("you will be known") appears to be a pious passive use to avoid a direct reference to God (that is, to avoid saying "God will know you"); compare 6a, where "heaven" is used as a circumlocution for God (cf. Matt 10:26; Luke 12:2). The meaning, stated directly, is, "God knows those who know themselves." "Know yourself" is a famous Greek aphorism that was inscribed in the Temple of Apollo at Delphi (Pausanius *Descr.* 10. 24.1). In the Greek context the saying urged knowledge of the self as a human being, but here the saying has a religious dimension: knowing yourself restores the knowledge of your divine origins (50). Compare *Teachings of Silvanus*: "the divine soul shares partly in this One [i.e., God]" and "partly in the flesh" (93:28–30). Those who do not "know themselves" are spiritually destitute ("impoverished"). Thus the way to knowledge of the divine comes by looking within. Compare a similar idea in Paul about the interior nature of the divine: Rom 8:9–11; 2 Cor 13:5; Gal 2:20, 4:19; and Col 1:19, 27; 2:9, and *Teach. Silv.* 116:27–117:5. Clement of Alexandria (late second century) makes a similar statement: "If one knows himself, he will know God, and knowing God he will be made like God" (*Paed.* 3:1). In *Thomas the Contender* it is said that Thomas "knows himself" and hence "knows the depth of everything" (*Thom. Cont.* 138:15–18). The Neoplatonist philosopher Plotinus (third century) described the experience of knowing God as an inner mystical ascent of the soul leading to a merging with the Supreme (i.e., the Good, the One; *Enn.* VI.9, 8–11). Plotinus's biographer, Porphyry, reported that during the years that he had been with Plotinus, he (Plotinus) had entered four times into union with the God "who has neither shape nor form." And Porphyry himself claimed to have entered once into union with God in his sixty-eighth year (Porphyry *Vit. Plot.* 23; Plotinus *Enneads* cxxi–cxxii). In the Hermetic tradition an individual became divine through "knowledge" (see the *Pr. Thanks.* 64:15–19). Pseudo-Dionysius the Areopagite (late fifth century) thought that regeneration brought about "in an unspeakable fashion, our divine existence." Divinization means having a divine birth. "No one could understand, let alone put into practice, the truths received from God if he did not have a divine beginning" (Dion. Ar. *e. h.* 392C: Luibheid, *Pseudo-Dionysus*).

For "the living Father," see saying 50. Poverty: see saying 29. For "knowing God," cf. John 17:3; 14:7; 16:3; Luke 10:22; 1 Cor 8:3; Gal 4:9; 1 John 4:6–7; 5:20; *Gos. Thom.* 69a. Cf. *Gos. Thom.* 111 and 70.

SAYING 4A

An elderly man will not hesitate to ask a seven-day-old child about the place of life, and he will live.

COMMENT

This aphorism has a familiar landscape with a contrast between an elderly man and a nearly newborn child. Old men are typically portrayed as the possessors of community wisdom, and tiny babies epitomize beginners on life's road. But in this case the world is turned on its ear, and the baby is portrayed as possessing unusual knowledge. Elders do not usually ask seven-day-old children serious philosophical and religious questions. For one reason, they cannot speak. The image presented in the saying is therefore a paradox. Where to find life, however, is a deadly serious issue. That issue begins this collection of sayings (saying 1). Spiritual wisdom is not found in the usual places but in the unusual (i.e., within oneself, saying 3b); it is not the common wisdom of the world (cf. 1 Cor 1:18–29). The saying reverses customary values. Little children are sometimes portrayed as possessing great insight, spiritual wisdom, or leadership ability (for example, Matt 18:1–5; Luke 2:41–47; Isa 11:1–5; *Apoc. Paul* 18:3–23).

A close parallel to saying 4a is found in Hippolytus *Ref.* 5.7.20 (see Stroker, *Extracanonical Sayings*, 95). In *Thomas* only the children (i.e., of the living Father) will come to know God's imperial rule (46). The Greek parallel to 4a is the same (Layton, *Nag Hammadi*, 115, 126). For "life" see saying 58.

SAYING 4B

Many first will be last, and they will become solitary.

COMMENT

The first half of this saying ("many first will be last") reduces by one strand a reversal saying of Jesus known in two parallel strands ("many first will be last and the last first," cf. Matt 19:30 and Mark 10:31). Matthew 20:16 and Luke 13:30 reverse the order (last/first and first/last. Similar sayings appear elsewhere (Luke 11:26; 18:14). In Thomas the saying becomes an antithetical parallelism: "the many first will be last, and they (the many that are last) will become solitary." Presumably, in saying 4b the many "first" represent those who hold popular religious views not shared by this text. Many (but not all!) of these will become "last" by coming to share the religious views of this text. The in-group view is represented by those who share the religious ideas of this text; they consider themselves judged last by others (that is, looked down on) because they are in the minority (sayings 23, 49, 75) and are hence out of the mainstream of religious thinking. Only those who become "last," that is, by sharing the views of this text, will merge with the One (sayings 22, 106, 108). Compare the discussion of saying 4b by Crossan (*In Fragments*, 46).

Singularity and unity are frequent themes in this text (sayings 11c, 16b, 22, 23, 48, 49, and 75) and in the New Testament as well (cf. John 10:16, 30; 14:8–11; 17:11, 20–23; Rom 12:4–5; 1 Cor 6:16–17; 10:17; 12:12–13, 26; Gal 3:28; Eph 2:14–18). For the "many"/"few" contrast, see saying 8. The Greek parallel is the same (Layton, *Nag Hammadi*, 115, 126).

SAYING 5

Discern what is in front of you, and everything concealed will become apparent.

COMMENT

Whoever possesses the spiritual insight represented by the little child in saying 4a will be able (spiritually) to discern the true nature of everything. The unenlightened person can only interpret reality's surface (cf. Luke 12:54–56 = Matt 16:2–3), but the one who has true spiritual discernment sees much more deeply (cf. 1 Cor 12:10). Compare Mark 4:22 = Matt 10:26 = Luke 8:17 = Luke 12:2; *Gos. Thom.* 6b). Mani (third century) quoted this saying of Jesus in reference to distinguishing the mystery of the light from the darkness (*Kephalia*, chapter 65: codex page 163:27–29: Gardner). The Greek parallel adds the statement from *Gos. Thom.* 6b (Layton, *Nag Hammadi*, 115, 126). See the discussion of sayings 6b, 17, 94, and 108.

SAYING 6A

His disciples asked him, "Do you want us to fast? How should we pray? Should we give alms? What should we eat?"
    Jesus replied, "Do not lie, and if you hate something, don't do it, for all things are evident to Heaven."

COMMENT

Jesus's response to the disciples' questions relating to religious ritual dismisses ritual acts as of no consequence. The disciples are told: be honest and true to themselves, for God knows the innermost secrets of the human heart. To perform ritual acts when the individual believes them to be meaningless is hypocrisy. Compare saying 14a, where ritual acts are harmful to the human spirit, and saying 53, where circumcision is dismissed as ineffectual, and saying 89, where ritual ablutions are ridiculed. Similar sayings are attributed elsewhere to Jesus (Matt 6:1–8, 16–18). But Jesus does not completely dismiss the ritual while *Thomas*, on the other hand, radicalizes spirituality and completely dismisses ritual acts.

"For all things are evident to Heaven": that is, to God. Compare the Matthean avoidance of the divine name, substituting "heaven" for "God" (for example, Matt 4:17 = Mark 1:14; Matt 5:3 = Luke 6:20; Matt 13:31 = Mark 4:30 = Luke 13:18). See also Hos 6:6; Mic 6:6–8. On food, see 1 Cor 8:8. Thus, being true to the enlightened inner self is more important than any ritual practice. Compare the fragmentary Greek parallel to 6a and 6b (Layton, *Nag Hammadi*, 116, 126).

SAYING 6B

What is hidden will be in plain sight, and what is covered will be stripped bare.

COMMENT

See saying 5, where all things are evident to the spiritually enlightened person. The saying about what is hidden being evident, in close connection to saying 6a, describes God's ability to see into the human soul, an ability also shared by the spiritually enlightened. Since the divine abides within each individual, naturally God knows our inner thoughts, and we know his. This saying, closely parallel to Luke 12:2, is associated with 6a almost as the authority for the position taken in saying 6a. See saying 62a, regarding the revealing of mysteries. See the discussion of sayings 17, 94, and 108.

SAYING 7

The lion a person devours is honored,
 for the lion becomes human.
If the lion does the devouring,
 the person is defiled,
 for the lion becomes the person.

COMMENT

A lion eaten by a human being is described as "honored," because it is humanized: that is, it participates in the nature of the human by being consumed. On the other hand, a person eaten by a lion is defiled, because the human being thereby participates in the lion's nature. The lion is a wild beast, proverbial for its courage and strength but also for its ravenous nature. In 1 Pet 5:8 the lion is a negative image; it is portrayed as "roaring," prowling about seeking to devour whomever it can. The principle underlying the saying is that human beings possess the capacities to be beastly or humane, and must struggle with the "beasts" within (*Teach. Silv.* 87:27–30; 107:17–25). Those who humanize their beast are fortunate, but if the beast gains the upper hand they are "defiled." Even the wise man can be controlled by the lion (*Sent. Sextus*, NHC 31:25–26 [saying 363b]); cf. also *Teach. Silv.* 105:26–34: It is possible to conquer the "wild beasts" and "lions" and become "human" through reasoning. On the struggle with the inner lion that pollutes, see the Manichaean psalm to Jesus 257:20–22 (Allberry, *A Manichaean Psalm Book*, 69; quoted in DeConick, *Original Gospel of Thomas*, 67). The Greek parallel to saying 7 is the same (Layton, *Nag Hammadi* 116–17, 127).

SAYING 8

The human being is like a shrewd fisherman who cast a net into the sea and drew it up full of small fish; among them was found one large, good fish. The shrewd fisherman threw all the small fish back and selected the large fish without a second thought. Better pay attention to this.

COMMENT

Human being: perhaps "true" human being (see King, *Gospel of Mary*, 59–62). This story shares a common heritage with Matthew's story of the seine net (Matt 13:47–48). Both of them appear to be different versions of a story by Aesop (see Perry, *Babrius and Phaedrus*, 9–10: "The Fisherman and the Fish"). The contrast in *Thomas* is between the many (small fish) and the one (large, good fish), rather than between small and large. Other stories in *Thomas* have a similar contrast between the many and the few (sayings 4b, 73–76a, and 107). The warning at the end of the story ("Better pay attention to this") is a floating saying in the canonical tradition (see Mark 4:9, 23; Matt 11:15; 13:9, 43b; Luke 8:8b; 14:35b; Rev 2:7, 11, 17, 29; 3:6, 13, 22; 13:9), and in *Thomas* (sayings 24, 63, 96). The saying alerts the reader that there is something unusual in the story.

On its surface the story appears to be a caricature of a shrewd fisherman who supposedly acts foolishly by selecting one large fish over a net full of small fish. Common wisdom would have opted for the many as opposed to the one—but why make a choice anyway? Why not keep them all? Thus the "shrewd" fisherman is foolish according to common wisdom, but at a spiritual level he has made the truly wise choice for the one over the many (saying 76a). The contrast at a deeper level is between common wisdom and unique spiritual discernment (cf. sayings 4 and 5 above). There are values in this world far exceeding the insight of common wisdom, but they can only be spiritually discerned (see saying 9).

SAYING 9

A farmer goes sowing by filling his hands with seeds and scattering them. Some seeds fall on the road, where the birds gather them. Others fall on rocks where they cannot strike root into the earth and hence do not send spikes up to heaven. Others fall into briar patches where they are choked, and eaten by worms. Others fall on good soil and shoot good spikes toward heaven: some sixty spikes per seed; others one hundred twenty spikes per seed.

COMMENT

Sowing, or broadcasting seed, is the common way of seeding fields in antiquity. According to this story, however, 75 percent of the time the seed fails to germinate, and where germination does occur the crop is only average (see the examples in Pliny *Nat.* 18.21.94–95). This story is also known in the canonical tradition (Mark 4:3–8 = Matt 13:3b–8 = Luke 8:5–8), where it is used to describe the limited success of Christian preaching in the first century because of the difficulties (Mark 4:14–20 = Matt 13:19–23 = Luke 8:11–15). Read against the image of farming as a positive figure for acquiring wisdom in Sir 6:19 ("Come to her [i.e., wisdom] like one who plows and sows, and wait for her good harvest. For in her service you will toil a little while, and soon you will eat of her produce"), this story denigrates human wisdom because of the farmer's marginal success (see the discussion of sayings 4a, 5, and 6b).

This narrative is treated in the Synoptic Gospels as an allegory (Mark 4:13–20 = Matt 13:18–23 = Luke 8:11–15), which is the primary way Jesus's parables were explained until the end of the nineteenth century (see saying 20), although Jesus himself was not an allegorist. The synoptic evangelists also often provided certain moral and theological summaries to the stories (see Hedrick, *Parables as Poetic Fictions*). The other stories (i.e., "parables") in *Thomas* are 8, 20, 21a, 57, 63–65, 76a, 96–98, 107, and 109.

SAYING 10

I cast fire upon the world—and observe—I tend it, until it blazes.

COMMENT

"Fire" is an image for what Jesus brings to the world. The saying is unclear as to what is being protected and what is expected to blaze. "It" could either be the world or the fire, or a combination of the two. A similar lack of clarity is found in a parallel saying in Luke 12:49. Fire is used elsewhere in *Thomas* as a positive image for a deed of the living Jesus. In saying 82, fire is identified as being "near Jesus" and synonymous with the imperial rule. In saying 16a, the living Jesus casts "divisions upon the earth" by means of fire, sword, and war, which describe the effects produced in those who discover the meaning of Jesus's words (saying 2).

In the Hebrew Bible, fire symbolized both the presence and protection of God (Exod 3:2–4; 13:21–22; Zech 2:5) as well as his judgment (Gen 19:24; Deut 4:23–24). Saying 10 makes a contrast between a small flame and a consuming fire; other sayings in *Thomas* make a similar contrast between small and large: sayings 20, 26, and 96. In the New Testament, fire and the Holy Spirit are the two characteristic features of the mission of the Christ as announced by John the Baptizer in Q (Matt 3:11–12 and Luke 3:16–17), and both words, *fire* and *spirit*, are part of the experience of the church at Pentecost (Acts 2:3–4). On the other hand, Mark's parallel summary of the characteristic mission of the Christ is that he will "baptize with the Holy Spirit" (Mark 1:8). But for *Thomas* the mission of the living Jesus is only to cast "fire upon the world" (that is, the "fire" of his words), which disturb (sayings 1, 2), divide, (saying 16a), and bring eternal life (saying 19c; cf. John 6:63, 68). For fire as an image for words, see Jer 5:14; 20:9; 23:29; Sir 48:1.

SAYING 11A

This heaven will pass away,
　and the one above it will pass away;
and the dead are not alive,
　and those who are alive will not die.

COMMENT

Two events are described as being certain in 11a: the destruction of the heavens (note the multiple heavens) and the current state of things in life. The saying comprises two loosely related parallel statements of two members each. The first saying is a synthetic parallelism, both members of which affirm the eventual obsolescence of the heavenly realms. Similar statements by Jesus (Mark 13:31 = Matt 24:35 = Luke 21:33; Matt 5:18; Luke 16:17, and *Gos. Thom.* 111), while not verbally exact, are conceptual parallels. Multiple heavens are a common feature of ancient cosmologies (cf. 2 Cor 12:1–2). The second half of 11a, describing the human realm from a religious perspective, is an antithetical parallelism. Each member in the second parallel statement asserts a religious certainty that is a common theme in *Thomas*: in the world, eternal life only abides in those whose lives have their source in the One-Who-Lives (37, 111); the "dead" are those who live as a part of the "world" (generally a negative concept in *Thomas*, see saying 21c) rather than out of the resources of the One-Who-Lives, who is the single source of true life (cf. Matt 8:22 = Luke 9:60; Eph 2:1, 5).

SAYING 11B

Previously you ate what was dead and made it alive. When you come into the light, what will you do?

COMMENT

The food we eat is first killed before we consume it (cf. saying 60), and then is integrated into our own living processes. Physical sustenance is a basic bodily need (cf. saying 7) and here epitomizes the human preoccupation with the physical world, for Jesus asks, but what will you do when you are enlightened? What will be the balance between spiritual realities and bodily realities? The second part of the statement encourages those who are enlightened to heed spiritual realities. The saying as interpreted here is similar to a statement attributed to the Naasanes: "If you ate dead things and made them living, what will you do if you eat living things?" (Hippolytus *Ref.* 5.8.32). The first part of saying 11b alludes to the physical world, and the second relates to spiritual realities. The expected answer to the question is, When I come into the light, I will eat living things. Compare *Gos. Phil.* 55:6–14: men formerly ate "dead things" like the animals, but when Christ came, he brought bread from heaven, or as John (6:51) puts it, "living bread."

SAYING 11C

On the day you were one, you became two. And becoming two, what will you do?

COMMENT

The likely context for this saying is the account of creation in Gen 2:4b–24. In that account the first human being, Adam, was a unified androgyne (meaning that Adam was both male and female), rather than being either male or female. The Creator's original separation of humanity (Gen 2:18–23) into two genders was a devolution from the original primordial unity of humanity (cf. saying 114). And the question becomes, how shall one regain that lost unity (cf. saying 4b)? The answer is found in saying 3b: by the mystical encounter with the One through knowing oneself and thereby restoring the original primordial unity of the self before creation. Becoming one with the One, or the One-Who-Lives, is a mystical union through which one becomes a child of the living Father (saying 3b) and is united with the other children of the living Father (4b). Similar mystical ideas of union with Christ and other believers are found in Paul (Rom 12:5; 1 Cor 6:17; 12:12–13).

SAYING 12

The disciples asked Jesus, "We know you are going away from us; who will be our leader then?"
Jesus replied, "When that happens, you will go to James the Just. For his sake heaven and earth came into being."

COMMENT

The disciples know that Jesus will leave them, and they ask about continuity of leadership. His departure need not be by crucifixion, for some radical Christian groups considered Jesus a "spiritual being"; that is, he only appeared to be a physical being (cf. 1 John 4:2–3; 1:1–4 ; John 1:14a, where he is argued to be "flesh"). At the end of his career he returned whence he came but was not crucified (*Apoc. Pet.* 82:17—83:15; *Treat. Seth* 55:14–56:19). The topic of the "departure" of Jesus is featured in the canonical gospels, where Jesus specifically predicts his imminent crucifixion (Mark 8:31; 9:30–32; 10:33–34) to prepare the disciples for his death. In John, on the other hand, his departure (like saying 12) is not directly linked to crucifixion (14:3, 18–19, 25; 16:5–7, 16–19, 25–28), and Jesus does not use his "departure" as an occasion to deliver instructions on his death. In saying 12 Jesus replies that when he has gone, they will go to James the Just (the brother of Jesus and a leader of the Jerusalem church; Eusebius *Eccl. Hist.* 2.23.4–18). Jesus replies to the question with a simple declarative statement rather than an imperative: Jesus is telling them what *will* happen, and not what they *should* do. The nature of James's leadership is temporary, as is made clear by the allusion to "heaven and earth coming into being because of him." For comparison, see 2 Esd 6:55–59 and 7:10–11, where God asserts that he made the earth for the Israelites. Both attributions constitute high praise indeed; but in sayings 11a and 111 the earth and heavens will pass away, and the association between James and the demise of the earth and heavens suggests the temporary character of James's leadership. Nevertheless, James was thought to hold an esteemed position in the diverse communities of the early Christian church (see Eusebius *Eccl. Hist.* 2.23; and *2 Apoc. Jas.* 55:15—57:11).

Leadership succession among Jesus's followers is handled in various ways with various apostles. For example, Peter is given the "keys of the kingdom" (Matt 16:13–20). Mary is cast as the disciple whom Jesus loved best, and who was a revelation bearer to the rest of the apostles (*Gos. Mary* 10:1–6). Even John the Baptist is given high praise (saying 46). In the Gospel of John, subsequent leadership is provided by the Comforter (14:15–17, 25–26; 15:26; 16:7–13). But in the *Gospel of Thomas* an immediacy of the divine exists within everyone who "lives in the living One" (see sayings 3b, 111).

SAYING 13

Jesus said to his disciples, "Compare me to someone; what am I like?"

Simon Peter said, "You are like a righteous angel."

Matthew said, "You are like a wise philosopher."

Thomas said, "Teacher, I do not have the words to say what you are like."

Jesus replied, "I am not your teacher, Thomas, for you have imbibed and become inebriated from the bubbling spring I measured out." And he took him aside, telling him three things.

When Thomas returned, his companions asked him, "What did Jesus say?"

Thomas replied, "If I tell you even one thing he said, you would stone me, and fire would come from the rocks and immolate you."

COMMENT

Angel: i.e., "messenger" (see the discussion at saying 88). A similar story appears in the canonical tradition in Mark 8:27-29 = Matt 16:13-20 = Luke 9:18-21. In saying 13, Jesus takes Thomas aside from the other disciples for special instruction because Thomas recognizes the essential difference of Jesus from everyone and everything. A similar situation occurs in the *Gospel of Judas*, where Judas is told five things: the nature of Gnostic reality, the truth about the creation of the world, the nature of humanity, the end of everything, and Judas's mission (*Gos. Judas* 35:6—36:9; 47:1-58, top). In the *Gospel of Mary*, Mary is given special instruction (*Gos. Mary* 10:9—17:7, virtually all of which is lost in lacuna), which the other disciples did not know. In the canonical tradition, Peter receives "the keys of the kingdom of heaven" because of his spiritual insight (Matt 16:16-19). In saying 13 the answers offered by the other disciples only reveal their spiritual blindness and the poverty of their spiritual insight. Because of his insight Thomas has achieved a certain parity with Jesus (see saying 108) and no longer needs to be instructed by him, because he has become intoxicated (i.e., spiritually enlightened; but see saying 28, where intoxication is a negative concept).

Unlocking the Secrets of the *Gospel according to Thomas*

In keeping with the secret character of *Thomas*, the three things Jesus told Thomas are not revealed (*Acts Thom.* 47 also mentions three sayings made to Thomas, but they are not disclosed). Compare, however, the three sayings in saying 50: knowledge of one's spiritual origin, knowledge of one's spiritual nature, and awareness of the inner presence of the divine. Such information is only for the "elect" and is scandalous for others to possess. Note also the three "hard" sayings of Jesus in saying 14a, which reject fasting, praying, and almsgiving. Stoning is a Jewish punishment for blasphemy (Lev 24:16; John 10:30–33). "Fire from the stones": cf. Judg 6:21, where the fire from the rock is a sign that the Lord had spoken to Gideon (Judg 6:17). In this case the threat of fire from the stones elevates the status of Thomas, and in the immediate context to saying 12 elevates the *Gospel of Thomas* over James. This story has a clear function in the *Gospel of Thomas*: it affirms Thomas's role as a reliable mystagogue and keeper of the mysteries from the living Jesus (saying 62a). Thomas does not tell the secrets indiscriminately.

SAYING 14A

By fasting you commit sin;
  for praying God will condemn you;
  giving alms will demonize your spirit.

COMMENT

In the canonical tradition Jesus seems to approve of the unpretentious practice of all three acts (Matt 6:1): when fasting, do not make a public display of it (Matt 6:16–18); when praying, pray in secret (Matt 6:5–6); when giving alms, give them in secret (Matt 6:2–4). But perhaps he does not completely approve of fasting (Mark 2:18–22). There is evidence that the early Christian communities practiced fasting (Acts 13:2–3; *Did.* 8.1). One group of interlocutors ("they" = the disciples?) in saying 104 seems to approve of fasting. Practices like these, however, can be hollow rituals, and doing them to be seen and praised by others damages your spirit. Likely for the same reason *Thomas* rejects these same specific ritual acts as harmful in saying 6a. In saying 53 circumcision is rejected as unnecessary. Piety in *Thomas* is an inner, spiritual matter and does not consist of public demonstrations of ritual, as it also applies in the *Shepherd of Hermas*, where "fasting" is interpreted in a spiritual way (Herm. *Sim.* 5.1.1–5; 5.2.5–8). Nevertheless, in saying 14a, such a categorical dismissal of traditional religious practices raises the possibility of hyperbole. Compare sayings 55, 101, 104, and Mark 9:43–47.

SAYING 14B

Wherever you travel, if the people of the land receive you, eat whatever they set before you and heal their sick.

COMMENT

This saying of Jesus is known in Luke 10:8–9a, where it appears in connection with instructions for missionary travel. Because of their Jewish roots, purity codes (what you should eat and with whom you should eat) were issues for early Christians as well: Gal 2:11–14; 1 Cor 8:7—13:1; 10:25–30; Rom 14:1–8; Col 2:16; Acts 10:1–34. For those who possess spiritual insight, however, such issues are of no consequence. People can eat without fear of ritual defilement, for true piety is a matter of the spirit. See sayings 6a, 14a, and 14c. The directive to heal the sick is found in Matt 10:1, 8 and Luke 10:9. This *Thomas* saying suggests the itinerant lifestyle of an early Christian prophet; see *Did.* 11–13. On healing the sick, see saying 19b.

SAYING 14C

What comes out of your mouth defiles you, not what goes in.

COMMENT

See sayings 14a, 14b, and sayings 45a and 45b. This saying, known in Matt 15:11 = Mark 7:15, stresses inner piety over public display. Breaking food taboos does not render a person unacceptable to God. People are impure because of what they are inside. Similar sayings attributed to Jesus in the canonical tradition are Mark 7:18–23 = Matt 15:17–20; Luke 6:45 = Matt 12:35.

SAYING 15

When you see one not born of woman, fall on your face and revere him; he is your Father.

COMMENT

Being "born of woman" characterizes the frailty of the human condition (cf. Job 14:1–5; 15:14; 25:4). No matter how worthy people are, they still fall short of divine righteousness (Matt 11:11 = Luke 7:28). Saying 46 describes John the Baptist as the greatest person "born of woman," but whoever "becomes a child" is greater than John (see saying 22 where the disciples claim to be "little children" and hence expect to enter the imperial rule). On the other hand, one not born of woman is self-originating, and hence the divine source of all (compare *Eugnostos* III,3:70:18—73:3; 74:20—75:23; also Rev 1:4, 8; 21:6; 22:13). The contrast between "born of woman" and "your Father" can scarcely be accidental in a text that finds a fatal flaw with humankind's origin in woman (cf. saying 114). In Matthew (1:18–21) and Luke (2:7) it is asserted that Jesus is "born of woman," which is exactly what Paul said about Jesus (Gal 4:4). John, on the other hand, says the "Word became flesh" (1:14), which is not quite the same thing as being "born of woman," or becoming human, for that matter. Hence saying 15 excludes the worship of Jesus; only the Self-Originating Father should be worshiped (see saying 50, where the Light originates through itself). Seeing the Self-Originating One is a divine encounter (cf. John 1:18), which Plotinus said happened within the individual soul (*Enn.* IV 8:1–11; V 1:10–12). See the comments under saying 3b.

SAYING 16A

Possibly people think I have come to bring peace to the world. They don't know that I have come to cast divisions on the earth—fire, sword, and war.

COMMENT

This saying is known in various forms in the canonical gospels: Matt 10:34 ("not peace but a sword"); Luke 12:51 ("not peace but division"). The language of the saying is paradox: an apparent contradiction or absurdity expressing a plausible truth in a shocking way. Hence, one must look past the literal meaning to a deeper meaning. Other similar sayings appear in the *Gospel of Thomas* (2, 6a, 10, 55, 101, and 105). Indeed many of the sayings in *Thomas* present a similar paradox; for example, 4a, 22, 24, 34, and 80. Saying 16a plays against a traditional Christian piety that viewed Jesus's message as one of peace, love, and harmony calling for assimilation of conventional values (for example, Rom 12:9–21; 13:8–10; 1 Cor 13:4–7; Jas 2:8–9; 1 John 4:7–11; 1 Pet 2:17; Gal 5:22–23; Eph 4:1–3). Saying 16a, on the other hand, understood the message of Jesus as shaking religious foundations and conventional piety, as the saying from the Hebrew Bible (Mic 7:6) in 16b clarifies: those who follow Jesus will experience disruption to their lives, separation from family and from the larger society.

SAYING 16B

Where five dwell in a house, three will be against two and two against three, father against son and son against father. Yet they will stand firm as the solitary.

COMMENT

Sayings 16a and 16b appear (with some differences) in a Q saying (Matt 10:34–36 = Luke 12:51–53) as a single saying of Jesus. But saying 16b is a significant close parallel to Mic 7:6, and hence is treated here as an independent saying. The Lukan version of the saying in Micah is the closest parallel to the combined saying, *Thomas* 16a and 16b. The saying in Micah describes the breakdown of the family in ancient Israel but is used by Matthew, Luke, and *Thomas* to describe the unrest caused by the preaching of Jesus (see sayings 2 and 10). Saying 16b closes with a positive affirmation. In spite of the disruption caused by the message of Jesus, there will be faithfulness to his cause.

The translation of the term *monachos* ("solitary" in the translation) has caused problems for translators. In the fourth century it was used almost exclusively for "monks," a designation for those who had withdrawn from normal society to live alone and apart from society (anchorites) or in communities of similar-minded people singularly devoted to the spiritual life. Prior to that time, the term served to describe single, individual, or unique things. It is used two other times in *Thomas*: in saying 49, where it is paired with the "elect" as those who will "find" the imperial rule, and in saying 75, where it is asserted that only the *monachos* will enter the bridal chamber. My translation of *monachos* as the "solitary" is intended to convey the idea of an exceptional person who remains single-mindedly devoted to God in spite of the difficulties and distractions of society (cf. Paul's discussion of marriage and singularity, 1 Cor 7:1–40, where it is clear that the preferred state is "singularity"). The Coptic expression translated "solitary" in sayings 4b and 23 (cf. also 22, 48) seems to be a synonym for *monachos*. On the basis of saying 23, it appears that the solitary one is also chosen or elected, but scholars disagree on this issue.

SAYING 17

What I give you has never been seen, heard, or touched; it has not even entered into the human mind.

COMMENT

This saying is known in a variety of Christian and non-Christian sources in antiquity; for example, it appears in Plutarch *Mor.* 17E (first century), where it is attributed to Empedocles, and in Sextus Empiricus's *Math.* 1.123 (second century). Hence it appears to be a traditional saying that did not originate with Jesus. See the collection of the parallels in Stone and Strugnell, *Books of Elijah*, 42–73. The earliest known use of the saying is by Paul (1 Cor 2:9); Paul introduces the quotation with a formula he uses to introduce quotations from the Hebrew Bible, although in the Hebrew Bible the saying does not appear as Paul renders it (but cf. Isa 64:4). The saying may be echoed in 1 John 1:1.

In this saying Jesus promises to disclose something totally new but does not hint at the content of the disclosure, as is consistent with the practice of *Thomas* (see sayings 1, 2, and 13). The promise in *Thomas* is consistent with Matt 13:35: "I will open my mouth in parables; I will utter what has been hidden since the foundation of the world" (a quotation of Ps 78:2). In 1 Cor 2:7 Paul echoes the idea of a novel disclosure from God: "We impart a secret and hidden wisdom of God decreed before the ages for our glorification." For Paul, the secret and hidden wisdom was what God accomplished through the death of Jesus (1 Cor 1:17–25). For *Thomas*, however, the novel revelation Jesus provides is not for public disclosure and is intended for only a select few (saying 62a), as Q suggested was the case (Matt 13:16–17 = Luke 10:23–24; cf. Mark 4:11–12). If the disclosure is totally unlike anything human beings have ever experienced, then they could not be expected to recognize its value except with spiritual insight (cf. 1 Cor 2:12–16). See the discussion of sayings 5, 6b, 94, and 108.

SAYING 18

The disciples said to Jesus, "Tell us about our future end."

Jesus replied, "So you understand all about the beginning and now look toward the end? You will find the end at the beginning. Whoever stands at the beginning is favored, for they will know the end and never die."

COMMENT

The disciples' question is unclear. Are they asking about the future of the Jesus movement, or are they asking about their own future deaths as individuals, i.e., how will they each die? Wanting to know how things turn out is natural human curiosity (cf. Ps 39:4). Similar questions about "ends," relating specifically to the destruction of the Jerusalem temple and the end of all things, appear in the canonical tradition (Matt 24:3 = Mark 13:3–4 = Luke 21:7). In *Gos. Thom.* 18 Jesus ignores what on the surface appears to be a natural question, particularly in light of saying 12, where Jesus is "going away." Instead Jesus gives a cryptic response, accusing the disciples of ignoring the more important question, that of understanding "the beginning." From Jesus's perspective, recovering the beginning brings both knowledge of the "end" and eternal life. It sounds like a nonsense answer. In the ancient world, however, the view of nature was cyclical: the earth renews itself every spring. The ancients did not think about human and natural history linearly as moving toward some final goal. In a cycle, the end of a phase includes the beginning of another; they lie at the same point. Hesiod (c. 700 BCE), the ancient Greek poet, described a succession of five ages to the world (golden, silver, bronze, demigods, and iron: *Works and Days* 109–201). In Hesiod's sequence the end and beginning of an age are the same point. Similarly the pre-Socratic Greek philosopher Anaximander (sixth century BCE) held that there were innumerable worlds coming into being and passing away (Simplicius *in Ph.* 5). Heraclitus (fifth century BCE) even said that beginning and end are common (to both directions), fragment 70 (Nahm, *Early Greek Philosophy*, 92). The Roman poet Virgil (first century CE) described the end of an old succession of generations and the beginning of a new generation (*Ecl.* 4, lines 4–5). In each case, the ancients thought cyclically; the beginning and the end coalesce. A similar association of beginning and end can be found in Jewish (Eccl 1:6, 9; 12:7; Isa 46:10; 2 Esd 6:1–6; 9:1–6) and Christian traditions (Origen *Princ.* 1.6.2): "For the end is always like the beginning"; i.e., where God was concerned, the beginning was simultaneous with the end. Perhaps the most significant coming together of beginning and end in the Christian tradition is found in the early Christian confession that God is "the alpha and the omega, the beginning and end" (Rev 1:8; 21:6), "the first and the last" (Rev 22:13; Isa 44:6).

Saying 18 in *Thomas* takes the ancient ideas of nature's annual renewal and ancient explanations of the nature of the cosmos and transforms them into a theological concept: a mystical return to the One, in whom reside both beginning and end (cf. 2 Esd 6:1–6). You must return, Jesus tells his disciples, to where all began—to the One-Who-Lives, from whence all came (sayings 3b and 11c), or as saying 49 says: the elect, solitary ones come out of the imperial rule and shall return there. The *Apocryphon of John* puts it this way: "It is because of you [the invisible Spirit] that Everything came into being and it is to you that Everything will return" (NHC II,*1*:9:8–10).

SAYING 19A

Favored is one who came into being before coming into being.

COMMENT

"Favored" i.e., the state of being approved or held in high regard (see the discussion in Hanson, "'How Honorable!' 'How Shameful!'"). The saying is a paradox, which is not an unusual form of speech for this text to use (see saying 4a). A paradox is an apparent self-contradiction or absurdity that seems to make no reasonable sense. Further, it is unclear whether the saying has in view one special person such as Jesus, who in the canonical tradition "preexisted" with God (John 1:1–3; 8:58) before "becoming flesh" (John 1:14), or whether it is a statement describing a specific group of people such as the solitary (saying 49). A saying attributed to Jeremiah by Irenaeus (*Epid.* 43) and Lactantius (*Inst.* 4.8) understands the following as a prophecy about Jesus: "Blessed is he who existed before he was made man." The precise quotation does not appear in Jeremiah, however; but cf. Jer 1:5. Read in the context of *Thomas*, however, saying 19a seems to refer to a larger group (but cf. saying 15), encompassing at the very least the elect, solitary ones (sayings 49 and 50), who came out of the imperial rule and will return there again. The same saying with a slight change in verb tense appears in *Gos. Phil.* 64:9–12: "Favored is the one who is, before coming into being; for the one who is, has been, and shall be" (cf. a version of the saying in Heb 13:8). What is unclear is whether everyone has a prior existence, or only the solitary. See the discussion of saying 42.

Translation and Commentary

SAYING 19B

Become my disciples, heed my words, and even the stones will serve you.

COMMENT

This saying has no exact parallel in the canonical gospels, but the spirit of the first part of the saying is found in John 8:31; 15:7, 14. The latter part of the saying affirms that disciples who heed the words of the living Jesus will have certain supernatural abilities—the stones will serve them. The general social context for this saying in antiquity was early Christian magic. "Magic refers to efforts to control supernatural forces for one's own ends by means that rest on some peculiar and secret wisdom" (Ferguson, *Backgrounds of Early Christianity*, 212). Even within the New Testament Jesus was thought to perform his "miraculous deeds" by magic (Mark 3:22; cf. Justin *1 Apol.* 30; Origen *Cels.* 1.38). In fact, certain sayings attributed to Jesus heard from a certain perspective provide the matrix for the practice of early Christian magic. Jesus tells his disciples if their faith were strong enough they could move mountains with a command (Matt 17:20 = Luke 17:6; *Thomas* 48, 106; see also 14b). Even Paul seems to know of such a tradition (1 Cor 13:2). The early oral Jesus tradition described magic-like manipulative acts performed by Jesus, such as a miraculous feeding (Mark 6:35–44), walking on water (Mark 6:45–52), cursing fig trees (Matt 21:19 = Mark 11:14, 20–21), and changing water into wine (John 2:1–11). Indeed early Christian tradition reports that Jesus told them whatever was asked in prayer and believed will happen (Mark 11:24 = Matt 21:22). And in a later tradition, Jesus tells the disciples that they will do "greater works than these" if they have faith (John 14:12). The idea that "stones" may be manipulated to serve is found in the Q tradition at Matt 3:9 = Luke 3:8, and Jesus was challenged to "change stones into bread" in the early Q legend of the temptation (Matt 4:3 = Luke 4:3). Compare the following early Christian texts related to the manipulation of nature by the followers of Jesus: Mark 16:17–18; Acts 3:6–8 (4:10); 9:36–41; 13:6–11; 19:11–12; 28:1–6; 1 Cor 12:10, 28; Jas 5:14–15.

SAYING 19C

Indeed you have five trees in paradise that do not move in summer and winter, and their leaves do not fall. Whoever knows them will never die.

COMMENT

The word "paradise" ("garden") is a Persian loan word in Greek, and is used in the Septuagint to translate "garden" (of Eden) in Gen 2:8–10, 16 (see Charlesworth, "Paradise"). In ancient Jewish thought, paradise becomes an ideal, heavenly place (2 *En.* 8:1–8; 4 *Ezra* 8:52), and in early Christian thought paradise is the heavenly destination of the believer (Luke 23:43; Rev 2:7; 2 Cor 12:4). In Gen 2:9 only two trees are named: the tree of life and the tree of the knowledge of good and evil, although it is clear that every tree "pleasant to the sight and good for food" also grows in paradise. Only one of these, however, brings immortality—the tree of life (Gen 3:22). First- or second-century *3 Baruch* (Slavonic) describes three trees (olive, apple, nut) and two vines (melon and grape) being planted in the garden (4:7–17). Ezekiel 31:8–9 names the following trees in the garden: the cedar, fir, and plane trees. Philo reports a tradition of six unusual trees growing in paradise (i.e., in the garden). He explains these trees allegorically as virtues that God plants in the rational soul, which lead to a life of virtue; they are life, immortality, knowledge, apprehension, understanding, and conception of good and evil (*Plant.* 36–37). In the third- or fourth-century *Pistis Sophia*, five trees are spread out in the Treasury of Light (book 2: chap. 86: MacDermot, *Pistis Sophia*, 191–95), and in the *Second Book of Jeu* (third or fourth century) the five trees of the Treasury of Light are described as "unmoved" (chapter 50: MacDermot, *Books of Jeu*, 119). In *Thomas* the trees also "do not move" in summer and winter.

What is it about these five unnamed trees in *Thomas* that the reader is expected to know? Why is the reader said to "have them"? The only hint is that the trees are perennial, enduring, and stable (cf. Zech 14:6–8), like the person who "delights" in the ways of God (Ps 1:1–3), or like God himself, who is frequently described in the Hebrew Bible as "my rock and fortress" (Ps 18:2; 31:3; 42:9; 71:3). One should likely think about the five trees as a Thomasine allegory (like Philo, and Paul in Gal 4:21–31), as resources accessible to the individual in the quest for immortality; for knowledge of these five trees results in immortality. Three other sayings in *Thomas* also promise immortality for different reasons: sayings 1, 18, and 85.

SAYING 20

The disciples said to Jesus, "The imperial rule of heaven, tell us what it is like."

He replied, "Like a mustard seed, the smallest of all seeds. When sown on tilled soil, it produces a large branch, which becomes a shelter for birds of the sky."

COMMENT

"Heaven," see saying 6a; "imperial rule of heaven," see saying 54. The imperial rule is featured also in sayings 3a, 22, 46, 49, 57, 76a, 82, 96–99, 107, 109, 113, and 114.

According to contemporary parables theory, Jesus's comparison is between God's imperial rule and the narrative, and not just between God's rule and the mustard seed. This brief story is also known from the canonical gospels (Mark 4:31–32 = Matt 13:31–32 = Luke 13:19), where it appears without interpretation, even though the early followers of Jesus tended to allegorize the parables or provide them with convenient morals (see saying 9). *Thomas* is different from the other three versions. In Mark the seed produces a shrub with large branches so that birds can build nests in its shade. In Matthew and Luke the seed produces a tree in whose branches birds build nests. In *Thomas* the earth produces a large branch providing shelters for birds (cf. Ezek 17:22–23; Dan 4:20–21). All four versions contrast the small beginning (the seed) and the large result (tree/large branches or branch).

Thomas, in keeping with the challenge for readers to "find the interpretation of the sayings," provides no interpretations for the stories. The Naasenes, a second- and third-century Gnostic sect, associated God's rule and the mustard seed as an indivisible point within the human being, known only to the spiritual (Hippolytus *Ref.* 5.9.6). As is clear from the history of parables interpretation, parables can mean almost anything the reader wants them to mean (see Hedrick, *Parables as Poetic Fictions*). For the contrast between large and small see sayings 8 and 96.

SAYING 21A

Mary asked Jesus, "What are your disciples like?"
   He replied, "Like little children who are squatters in a field that does not belong to them. When the owners come, they will say, 'Give us back our field.' They disrobe in their presence to release it to them, and give the field back."

COMMENT

There are no parallels to this story in the canonical gospels, but it is distinguishable as a separate saying by its character as a self-contained story and by the fact that 21b–21d form a series of sayings reported individually in different contexts in the canonical tradition. The identity of Mary is uncertain (cf. saying 114). Early Christian tradition knew of several persons named Mary (John 11:1; Luke 2:16; Mark 16:1; Matt 28:1; John 19:25; Acts 12:12; Rom 16:6; Luke 8:2–3). For the disciples as children, see sayings 4a, 22, and 46, and Matt 18:2–4; 19:13–15; Mark 10:13–15; Luke 18:15–17.

There are no known parallels to the idea that one demonstrably abdicates a legal claim by removing one's clothes (but cf. the role of sandals in legal responsibility in ancient Israel: Deut 25:5–10; Ruth 4:7–9). In *Thomas* the divesting of clothing is associated with seeing the son of the Living One (saying 37). And similarly the Naasenes are reported to have said of those who arrive at the "gate of heaven, the house of God," where God dwells alone, that they must lay down their clothing and become bridegrooms, being rendered wholly male (saying 114) through the virgin spirit (Hippolytus *Ref.* 5.8.44). Irenaeus interprets the "divesting" as an act in which the "spiritual" divest themselves of their souls before entering the bridal chamber (cf. 75, 104) in order to become intelligent spirits (Irenaeus *Haer.* 1.7.1; Foerster, *Gnosis*). On the other hand, elsewhere the concept of "stripping" is related to the physical body and the donning of a spiritual garment (2 Cor 5:1–4; 1 Cor 15:42–50; *Gos. Phil.* 56:26—57:22). Under both explanations the narrative is converted into an allegory (see 9, 20), and the narrative as allegory casts the disciples as aliens in a foreign land (see saying 50).

SAYING 21B

Therefore, a homeowner who knows the thief is about to come remains awake until the thief comes so as to prevent the break-in and loss of property.

COMMENT

If this saying is deliberately appended to saying 21a as an interpretation ("therefore" is not in the canonical parallels), then it is the only narrative in *Thomas* that has such an appended explanation (see sayings 9 and 20); but compare the debated ending to 64a in 64b, and the discussion of sayings 74 and 75. *Thomas* 21b is a Q tradition (Matt 24:43 = Luke 12:39); in Q it is explained as a warning about the unexpected coming of the Son of Man. It also appears in *Pistis Sophia* (book 3: chap. 121: MacDermot, *Pistis Sophia*, 308), where it seems to relate to an individual's unexpected death ("their time of coming forth from the body," book 3, chapter 120: MacDermot, *Pistis Sophia*, 308). A doublet of saying 21b is found in saying 103, where it appears as a macarism. A related saying is found in 35.

Saying 21b appears to be common wisdom: who would not act resolutely to prevent a thief from breaking into the family home in the middle of the night? The answer is no one. But the wise action of the homeowner is predicated on prior knowledge of the break-in. Hence the saying commends uncommon perception and at the same time condemns ignorance (i.e., lack of knowledge). In *Thomas* the precarious nature of the inner person cannot be corrected by human wisdom or resolute action, but only by spiritual insight. See the discussion of sayings 3b, 4a, and 8; and note similar ideas in sayings 21d, 51, 63, 67, and 97. In the canonical tradition compare Eph 3:2–6 and 1 Cor 2:7–15.

SAYING 21C

Watch out for the world, and prepare yourself with great strength so that thieves will not exploit your weakness, because they will seize the advantage, as you expect they will.

COMMENT

In *Thomas* the term "world" is not neutral (see saying 56; a similar use is found in John: 1:10, 29; 7:7; 14:16–17; 15:18–19; 17:14, 16; 18:36; and Paul: Rom 11:15; 1 Cor 1:20; 3:19; 2 Cor 5:19; see also Jas 1:27). It represents a construct of life diametrically opposed to the imperial rule of God (sayings 27, 28, 64a, 64b). The world's structures are opposed by the living Jesus (sayings 10, 16, and 28) because the world corrupts those who live under its influence (saying 27); but escape from its control is possible (sayings 28, 51, 56, 80, and 110). This saying has no parallels in the Jesus tradition. It is a warning to the disciples of the living Jesus. They are still at risk; as long as they are in this life, they potentially can fall under the influence of the world. *Thomas*'s representing the world as adversarial and opposed to the imperial rule encourages the reading of 21c as an allegorical interpretation of 21b. Saying 21b is a bit of common wisdom: common sense dictates that one should be prepared for the attack, but 21c explains the situation as a spiritual threat. Hence, disciples expect to be under threat from the wiles of the world and must prepare themselves with (spiritual) strength. Similar ideas are found in other early Christian texts (Rom 13:12; 1 Cor 7:5; 1 Thess 3:5; Eph 6:11–13). The author of *Diognetus* (second century) puts it this way: "Christians dwell in the world, but are not of the world" (6:3; cf. John 17:11, 14, 16). "Exploit your weakness"; literally: "Find a way to come to you."

SAYING 21D

You should have among you a person of skilled knowledge. When the fruit was ripe, he came quickly with his sickle in hand and reaped it. Better pay attention to this.

COMMENT

What I have treated here as a single saying in 21d may well be three separate sayings: (1) "you should have among you a person of skilled knowledge"; (2) "when the fruit was ripe, he came quickly with his sickle in hand and reaped"; (3) "better pay attention to this." The last phrase is a well-known saying used in various contexts in early Christian literature (see saying 8). The first phrase has no verbal parallels in early Christian literature, but there are conceptual parallels (Jas 3:13–18; 1 Cor 12:8, 10). The second phrase has a close parallel in Mark 4:29. The language is close enough to regard 21d (phrase b) as a variant of Mark 4:29. Scholars have treated the phrases in 21d differently. For some, all three are regarded as separate sayings; for others 21d (phrase a) is regarded as the conclusion to 21c. I regard all three phrases of 21d as a composite statement related to the previous saying. In early Christian texts the harvest theme in 21d (phrase b) is treated as a judgment saying (cf. Matt 3:12; Rev 14:15–16, 18–19; see also Joel 3:13). But *Thomas* presents the second phrase of 21d as an example of what it means to possess skilled knowledge. Knowing both the precise moment for action and how to act are the marks of a disciple possessing skilled knowledge (compare Matt 13:51–52; Luke 12:56; Col 4:5–6).

Translation and Commentary

SAYING 22

Jesus saw children nursing and said to his disciples, "Those who enter the imperial rule are like nursing children."

They said, "Since we are children, then, shall we enter the imperial rule?"

Jesus replied:

"When you make the two into one,
the inner as the outer,
the outer as the inner,
what's above like what's below;
when you make male and female into the solitary,
so that the male is no longer male
and the female no longer female;
when you make eyes out of an eye,
and a hand to replace a hand,
a foot to replace a foot,
and an image to replace an image,
then you will enter into the imperial rule."

COMMENT

The disciples ask Jesus a strange question: will they too enter into the imperial rule? The question is strange since one would expect disciples already to be under the imperial rule. Jesus had already described them "like little children" (saying 21a). But they were apparently thinking of a future postdeath experience that involved the ultimate state of the blessed. *Thomas* generally portrays the disciples in a negative fashion—asking the wrong question, giving the wrong answer, or thinking at a natural level while Jesus is thinking at a different, spiritual level (sayings 6a, 12, 18, 20, 24, 37, 43, 51–53, 60, 99, 113, and 114; cf. 79a). Rarely are they portrayed in neutral fashion (saying 72). They are portrayed as the disciples in the Gospel of Mark are described (for example, Mark 8:14–21). Some translators render the question like this: "shall we then as children enter into the imperial rule?" And then this version of the disciples' question is compared to the question of Nicodemus, who misunderstands what it means to be "born anew" (John 3:4). That is, in this saying from *Thomas*, the disciples think they must actually revert to being children again, just as in John's gospel Nicodemus thinks it necessary to undergo physical birth a second time. The *Gospel of Thomas*, like the Gospel of Mark (9:47; 10:15, 25; 12:34), uses spatial language to describe how one relates to the rule of God: one enters into (sayings 22, 99, and 114), finds (sayings 27 and 49), knows (saying 46), possesses (saying 54), or is far from (saying 82) the imperial rule. But it is clear in *Thomas* that God's rule is not "out-of-this-world," but rather a particular dynamic experience, capable of being realized in this life (sayings 3a, 113). Thus, surprisingly, the force of Jesus's statement is that being a disciple is not enough. Even disciples must comply with the requirements set out in his answer to the disciples' question.

The first line of the response to the question is the theme for the first seven lines in the poetically arranged part of the saying above—i.e., making the two into one (see sayings 4b, 106, and 108). The inner and the outer (saying 89) must be one (saying 3a); above and below must become one; male and female must be a single one (saying 114). Variations of the contrasts in these lines of the saying, with the goal of producing a unity out of the opposites, are widely reported as a saying of Jesus (see Stroker, *Extracanonical Sayings*, 12–16). Lines 8–11 of the poetically arranged text, however, are not opposites, and one of these lines (line 8) actually contradicts the dominant idea of the first seven lines (i.e., making two into one) by commending the turning of one eye into multiple eyes. These later lines basically replace one thing with another (see *Ep. Pet. Phil.* 136:5–15).

Mythically, becoming one is how one regains the original primordial state before differentiation of the genders takes place (see *Corp. herm.* 1.17–18). In Gen 2:21–23 the first human being is created as an androgynous whole and then differentiated into male and female. Line 5 of the poetic text in this saying seems to evoke that situation by having the union of male and female produce "the solitary," a special class of human being chosen by God (see sayings 23, 75, and 4b). In the social context, marriage and sexual union were conceived in early Christian communities as "becoming one flesh" (Matt 19:4-6 = Mark 10:6-8; Eph 5:31-32; 1 Cor 6:15–16). In the community context, the goal is the obliteration of social classes: there is neither Jew nor Greek, slave nor free, male nor female; all are one in Christ Jesus (Gal 3:28–29). *Thomas* expresses it as "two making peace with each other in this one house" (saying 48). See the brief commentary on saying 22 in *2 Clem.* 12:2–5.

SAYING 23

I will choose you: one from a thousand and two from ten thousand, and the chosen ones will stand firm being solitary.

COMMENT

The choice of solitaries (see saying 49) is extremely selective: one in a thousand and two in ten thousand (cf. Matt 22:14). They are a minority but will endure unified (on singularity and/or "solitary," see saying 4b). The numbers used in the saying (Deut 32:30; Eccl 7:28; 1 Sam 18:7; Ps 91:7; Mic 6:7), and even the saying itself (see Stroker, *Extracanonical Sayings*, 186–87), have a proverbial character. On "standing firm," see sayings 16b, 18, 28, and 50.

SAYING 24

His disciples said, "Show us where you are, for we must seek that place."

He replied, "If you have ears, listen up: Light exists in an illuminated person, and it lights up the entire world. Darkness persists when no one lets their light shine."

COMMENT

The answer of Jesus to the disciples' very strange question demonstrates the spiritual insensitivity of the disciples (for another strange question from the disciples, see saying 22). At the time they ask the question, Jesus is right there in front of them (cf. sayings 52 and 91). How could they not know "where he was," since his "light" (saying 77a) illuminated all about him (saying 33b)? Light and darkness constitute an ethical contrast in *Thomas*; the light is positive (cf. sayings 61b, 11b, and 50), and darkness, as the opposite of light, negative. But it is not quantified beyond the contrast in *Thomas*. Probably one should think of "light" in terms of the purpose of the living Jesus in the world (see sayings 28, 10, 16a, 17), but *Thomas* does not openly tell the reader what that purpose is. The ethical contrast between light and darkness (cf. 61b) is a well-known theme in other early Christian texts (Matt 6:22–23 = Luke 11:34–35; Luke 1:78–79; John 1:5; 3:19–21; 8:12; 12:35–36, 46; Rom 2:19; 2 Cor 6:14; 1 John 1:5–7).

The translation above takes "light" as the subject of the expression "light up the entire world," but it is possible that "an illuminated person" is the subject (that is, "light exists in an illuminated person, and that person lights up the entire world"). The Greek fragment has the same obscurity (Layton, *Nag Hammadi*, 117, 127). On the light existing within, see saying 3b.

For the floating saying "If you have ears, listen up," see saying 8, where it is translated "Better pay attention to this."

SAYING 25

Love your brother like your own self; take care of him as you do the pupil of your eye.

COMMENT

Because of the voice in which this writer presents the sayings (i.e., in the voice of Jesus), it is difficult to see in the text concrete evidence of a later community for which the text was produced. There are hints, however; and in saying 25 the word "brother" is one of these hints (see also sayings 26 and 99). In the early Christian communities, love for the "brother," apparently a collective word for the other members of the community, including both men and women (Rom 13:8a; 1 John 2:10; 3:10; 4:21), was a standard feature of community life. Paul cited the biblical injunction for the Israelite to love the "neighbor" (Lev 19:18, 33–34), which meant a fellow Israelite (Deut 15:3–4), and at that time the word "neighbor" signaled an ethnic distinction. It is possible, however, that Paul broadened the Hebrew Bible's concept of "love of neighbor" to include fellow human beings (Rom 13:9–10; Gal 5:14), as James seems to do (2:8). Jesus also is credited with quoting Lev 19:18 (Matt 22:39 = Mark 12:31 = Luke 10:27). What was most distinctive about Jesus, however, was his saying about love for an "enemy" (Matt 5:43–44 = Luke 6:27–28; cf. John 15:13; Rom 12:20). *Didache* 2:7 says hate no one, some reprove, and for some pray, and "some you shall love more than your own life." The lost *Gospel of the Hebrews* is cited as saying, "never be glad except when you look at your brother or sister with love" (Miller, *Complete Gospels*, fragment 7). The *Epistle of Barnabas* (first or second century) says, "Love your neighbor more than your own life" (19:5), and love "as the apple of your eye" all who speak the word of the Lord to you (19:9). *Thomas*, however, is more like the Johannine letters, which seem clearly to focus love on the members of the community.

SAYING 26

You can find a sawdust speck in your brother's eye
  but fail to notice the plank in your own.
When you extract the plank from your eye,
  then you can see to remove the speck from your brother's eye.

COMMENT

On the "brother," see saying 25. Saying 26 is a shorter version of the Q saying in Matt 7:3–5 = Luke 6:41–42. The statement is hyperbole—exaggeration for effect. Stated in discursive language, the saying describes hypercritical persons being completely unaware of their own personal failings. For an affirmative statement of the same principle see Phil 2:3. In the early Christian communities, believers were advised to consider their own shortcomings (Rom 2:1; 12:16; 14:10; 2 Cor 13:5; Gal 5:26; 6:1–3) in their treatment of other members of the community (Rom 15:1–2; 1 Cor 8:10–12; Gal 6:1; 1 Thess 5:14–15; Jas 4:11). Only the last phrase is preserved in the Greek fragment (Layton, *Nag Hammadi*, 118, 127).

SAYING 27

If you don't fast from the world, you will never discover the imperial rule. You must make the Sabbath a Sabbath if you would see the Father.

COMMENT

Thomas rejects fasting as a harmful religious exercise (6a, 14a, 104), but here uses the term "fasting" metaphorically (compare a similar interpretation of fasting in Herm. *Sim.* 5.5.1–5). The literal meaning of the verb "to fast" is abstaining from all food—to eat nothing. In saying 27, however, one "fasts from the world," meaning that one abstains from involvement with the "world," which is a negative concept in Thomas (saying 21c). "To fast from the world" means not conforming to its values (cf. Rom 12:2) and not being under its influence (Col 2:20; Jas 1:27; 1 John 2:15). This metaphorical use of fasting is common in Christian antiquity (for parallels to the expression, see Stroker, *Extracanonical Sayings*, 235–37). Note the parallelism of the saying (cf. sayings 6b, 25, 81, and 82 for other parallelisms): "fasting from the world" is equivalent to "mak[ing] the Sabbath a Sabbath"; "discovering the imperial rule" is equivalent to "seeing the Father." Hence one discovers the imperial rule by a cessation of involvement with the world. In the Hebrew Bible, the Sabbath is the seventh day of the week, which was conceived as a day of rest and cessation from labor (Gen 2:2–3) and so observed in ancient Israel (Exod 16:25–30; 23:12; 34:21). Most of the early followers of Jesus observed Sunday as their day of worship (Acts 20:7; 1 Cor 16:2; *Did.* 14; *Gos. Pet.* 9: Miller, *Complete Gospels*, 405; Justin, *1 Apol.* 67), but some conceived a "Sabbath rest" to describe eternal rest (Heb 3:16—4:10). On the "imperial rule," see sayings 20 and 22; for "seeing the Father," see John 6:46; 14:9. For "seeing God," see Matt 5:8; John 1:18; 3 John 11. The Greek fragment of this saying is particularly close (Layton, *Nag Hammadi*, 118, 127).

SAYING 28

I stood in the midst the world, appearing to them in flesh. I found them all inebriated and none among them thirsty. My soul was pained for humanity's children because their minds are blind, and they do not see that having come empty into the world, they are also seeking to go out of the world empty. But now they are inebriated. When they shake off their wine, will they then change their minds?

COMMENT

This saying has some affinities with traditional early Christian ideas about Jesus; for example, the language echoes certain New Testament concepts and language: "stand in the world" (John 10:36; 12:46; 16:28; 17:18; 18:37; Heb 10:5), "in flesh" (John 1:14; 1 Tim 3:16), "appeared" (Heb 9:26), "inebriated" (Rev 17:2), "thirsty" (Matt 5:6; John 7:37), "blind in mind" (John 12:40; Rom 1:21, 2:5; 2 Cor 3:15–16, 4:4), "empty" (1 Tim 6:7). But taken as a whole, the pronouncement affirms things about Jesus and his mission that are radically different. The pronouncement seems to fit into a different thought-world; compare the proclamation to humankind in *Corp. herm.* 1.27. In *Thomas* the living Jesus comes "in flesh"; that is, he is not really human. He is an alien to the world and its ways. This claim about Jesus is similar to John's claim about Jesus: that he "*became* flesh" (John 1:14), which is something different from claiming that he is "human." Nevertheless, John's claim is similar to the early Christian hymn or creed in Phil 2:5–11. The "world" must be understood as comprising "all children of humanity," who are specifically addressed throughout the saying: note the parallelism of the first statement: "stand in the *world*, and appeared to *them*."

Emptiness is a negative concept in *Thomas* (saying 97), as is poverty (sayings 3b and 29), but it is never explained (in keeping with saying 1). Likely, however, emptiness is the absence of what the living Jesus gives (17). Saying 28 avoids describing that for which humanity's children did not thirst. It is presumably the content of the message that Jesus had presented to them (see sayings 16a and 16b for the character of his message). It is clear, however, that being "empty" of what Jesus gives is dangerous (saying 70). For inebriation used in a positive sense, see saying 13.

The last line of saying 28 is usually translated as a rhetorical statement rather than a question: i.e., "When they shake off their wine, they will then change their minds." But given the low number of the chosen in this text (sayings 23, 62a, and 75; cf. sayings 8, 9, and 49), my translating it as a statement would imply too much optimism by the living Jesus.

The last part of the Greek fragment is in lacuna (Layton, *Nag Hammadi*, 118–19, 127). "Empty into the world; empty out of the world"; compare Job 1:21. Humanity's children are the children of Adam after he was devolved into two separate genders: see saying 106, where Adam's children are descendents of Adam before the devolution into two separate genders.

SAYING 29

If flesh came into being to accommodate spirit—
   what a wonder!
And if spirit came into being for the body,
   it is beyond amazing.
But I am astounded at how such great wealth resides in such poverty.

COMMENT

This saying addresses anthropology and anthropogony: study of the origin and development of humankind. This saying asserts that a human being is a duality of flesh and spirit, which together compose a body. In ancient Hebrew thought, the human being is a singularity: Adam was created as a "living being," a unified entity of soil and the breath of God (Gen 2:7). In Greek thought, human beings were dualistically conceived: a material/mortal part (flesh/body) and an immortal/divine part (spirit/soul), both of which were distinct (Plato *Tim.* 9–13). Among early Christian writers the situation is not as neat. Paul thought of a human being as a unity in the ancient Hebrew way and used the term "body" to describe the whole human being (Rom 6:12; 12:1), but he also uses other language to describe aspects of the human being: "soul," "spirit," "mind," "conscience," "heart," and "flesh" (see Bultmann, *Theology*, 1:187–269). In Gnostic thought, speculation on human origins and constitution is a significant issue (see Rudolph, *Gnosis*, 88–113). In a recently discovered text the *Gospel of Judas*, for example, anthropogony is part of the revelation given by Jesus to Judas (Coptic pages 52–53); cf. *Ap. John* II,1:15:1—23:35. Human makeup is also a concern in Hermetic texts (*Corp. herm.* 1.15, 18; 7.2–3; 10.15–18; 12.1–4; Copenhaver, *Asclepius* 8–10).

In *Gos. Thom.* 29 the living Jesus focuses on the relationship of the flesh, or the body, and spirit. What is the reason and order of their origin? It would be a marvel if the only reason that flesh or body was generated was as a receptacle for spirit, and even more surprising if spirit originated just to animate the body. In Gen 2:7 the creation of Adam's body preceded the animating breath of God (as is also the case in *Orig. World* 115:3—116:8). But in *Hyp. Arch.* 88:1–15 the spirit pre-existed the creation of Adam (87:11–20), as did the spirit in Herm. *Sim.* 6:5. The living

Jesus stresses the abject poverty of the material and the marvelous value of the spirit, and in a sense rejects the first two positions in the apparent debate about the value of the flesh or the body and the spirit. Similar ideas about the value of the spiritual over the material appear in Paul (2 Cor 8:9; Rom 8:13; 1 Cor 15:50 [spiritual body over fleshly body]; *Gos. Phil.* 56:20–26). In the *Gospel of Thomas*, the astonishing thing for the living Jesus is the presence of spirit in matter, since the two are irreconcilable (sayings 87 and 112).

For comments on poverty, see sayings 3b and 28 ("empty"), saying 41 ("little taken"), and saying 97 ("empty"). For comments on great wealth, see saying 85. Very little is left of the Greek fragment (Layton, *Nag Hammadi*, 119, 127).

Translation and Commentary

SAYING 30

Where there are three gods,
  they are gods.
Where there are two or one,
  I am with it (i.e., the one).

COMMENT

The saying is obscure, and possibly corrupt. The Greek fragment (P. Oxy. 1) containing this saying reads: "Where there are three, they are without God, and where there is one alone, I say that I am with him" (Layton, *Nag Hammadi*, 119, 127). A resumptive ⲘⲘⲀⲨ ("there") is regularly used in *Thomas* following ⲘⲀ ("place"; see the indices in Layton, *Nag Hammadi*, 267-68) and should be restored in saying 30 as follows: ⲤⲚⲀⲨ Ⲏ ⲞⲨⲀ <ⲘⲘⲀⲨ> ("two or one in the place there") as it appears in the first half of saying 30. The expression is usually not translated. To saying 30 the Greek fragment immediately adds a saying (appearing in the Coptic text as 77b): "Lift up the stone and there you will find me; split the wood and I am there" (Attridge "Greek Fragments" 119–20, 127; but compare DeConick, *Original Gospel of Thomas*, 36–37).

Can any sense be gleaned from the Coptic? In general, the Coptic saying seems to contrast two different locations: where multiple gods exist, and where the living Jesus is. The first part of the saying is the only place in *Thomas* that evokes a religiously polytheistic world, and it simply acknowledges the dominion of multiple gods where they are recognized as such. The second half of the saying associates the living Jesus with "it" (that is, with "the one" in the previous expression, just as the Greek fragment renders the saying). For multiple gods, see Ps 82:6 and John 10:34.

SAYING 31

Prophets are not acceptable in their villages;
  physicians don't medically treat those who know them.

COMMENT

The saying is composed of twin antithetical statements with the same general exaggerated meaning: "familiarity breeds contempt." Hence they are likely traditional proverbs rather than aphorisms (see sayings 34, 47a). An aphorism is a terse statement of a principle or precept whose meaning is unclear on the surface (see saying 62b). A proverb is a short pithy saying that embodies community wisdom, whose sense is immediately obvious at a literal level (see saying 47a). The first statement has parallels in the Jesus tradition (Luke 4:24 = Mark 6:4 = Matt 13:57 = John 4:44). The second does not have a precise parallel, but a negative sentiment about physicians is found in Luke 4:23. Each statement reflects the disappointment of the living Jesus over his reception, as it is reflected in saying 28. In the context of the canonical gospels, both statements would describe the general lack of acceptance of Jesus and his message. For the close Greek parallel, see Layton, *Nag Hammadi*, 120, 127.

SAYING 32

A fortified city built atop a high mountain cannot fall, nor will it be concealed.

COMMENT

The saying (see the Greek fragment in Layton, *Nag Hammadi*, 120, 127) has a close parallel in Matt 5:14b, where it appears in synonymous parallelism to the lamp under a bushel basket (i.e., neither the city nor the lamp is hidden). This latter saying (Matt 5:15) is also found in *Gos. Thom.* 33b as a separate saying; *Gos. Thom.* 32 is a proverb.

The first assertion about the city (that it cannot fall) is an exaggeration describing invincibility, and is not true (see, for example, Josephus on the fortifications at Gamlah and its defeat: *J.W.* 4:1.1–10). The second assertion on the visibility of the city is generally true; it would be difficult to hide a walled city on a hilltop. The first assertion about the invincibility of the city is unique to *Thomas* and has no parallel among known Jesus sayings. How the readers of *Thomas* may have understood the saying hinges on the contexts in which they read it, a circumstance that also applies to most of Jesus's sayings. In *Thomas* the two assertions about the city should likely be read with reference to the following: invincibility, saying 35; visibility, sayings 5, 6b, 24, 33a and 33b, and 108.

SAYING 33A

Whatever you hear in your ear, proclaim from your roof.

COMMENT

Literally the Coptic scribe has written "What you will hear in your ear, in the other ear proclaim from your roof." This nonsensical reading is probably due to a scribal error. Likely the scribe has mistakenly written "in your ear" twice (i.e., a dittography), and mistakenly reversed two Coptic letters in the second iteration (i.e., a metathesis), which changes the second iteration of "in your ear" to read "in the other ear." The Greek version of the saying is too fragmentary to be of help in clarifying the difficulty (Layton, *Nag Hammadi*, 121, 127).

The saying is paralleled in a Q tradition: Matt 10:27 = Luke 12:3, where Jesus says, "What you hear in the ear (i.e., whispered) proclaim on the housetops" (Matt 10:27); "What you have told to the ear (i.e., whispered) in private rooms shall be proclaimed upon the housetops" (Luke 12:3). In other words, it is a private communication that becomes a public announcement—just as it appears in *Thomas*. This saying is the only clear indication in *Thomas* that followers of the living Jesus have a responsibility for actively proclaiming their faith, though it seems clear that they should do so (sayings 6b, 32, and 73). This saying appears to contradict 62a, where the mysteries of Jesus are not presented to the public, but as sayings 1 and 2 point out, the mysteries are given to those who seek them. In other early Christian texts, similar directives for evangelism appear, and the directives are more frequent than appear in *Thomas*: Matt 28:19–28; Mark 16:15–16; and Acts 1:8. The early followers of Jesus had the responsibility to be active witnesses for their faith: Acts 22:13–16; 26:12–18; Rom 15:18–20; Gal 1:18–24; 1 Thess 1:8–9.

SAYING 33B

No one lights a lamp and puts it under a basket or in a concealed place, but a lamp is placed on a lamp stand so that everyone who enters and leaves can see by its light.

COMMENT

This saying is found in the canonical gospels in three different but clearly related versions (Matt 5:15 = Mark 4:21 = Luke 8:16; Luke 11:33). The *Thomas* saying has the ring of common wisdom, but compare Funk et al., *Five Gospels*, 492. The living Jesus uses language appropriate to lamps to describe something else, but precisely what he (and the historical Jesus) was talking about through this indirect statement is unclear. The synoptic writers usually embed discrete Jesus sayings in literary contexts, which help in clarifying how they understood them. In this case, a series of sayings (32, 33a, and 33b) appear linked in *Thomas*, apparently to clarify that disciples have a responsibility to proclaim their faith (sayings 33a, 24), but only within certain constraints (saying 62a). In the early Christian churches there appear to be no constraints, however; the mystery of the gospel is an open secret (Rom 16:25–26; Eph 6:18–19; Col 1:24–28; but see saying 62a). Clement of Alexandria (second and third century), citing this saying by Jesus, appears to be closer to the understanding of *Thomas*: "neither prophecy nor the Savior himself announced the divine mysteries simply so as to be easily comprehended by all and sundry" (*Strom.* 6.15.124.5–6). It is notable, however, that although Jesus says "no one lights a lamp and puts it under a basket," Thomas does precisely that.

SAYING 34

If someone blind leads another who is blind, they both fall into a pit.

COMMENT

This saying is closely parallel to a Q saying appearing in Matt 15:14. In Luke 6:39 the Q saying appears as a question. The saying is an aphorism whose literal meaning is unclear, since blind folk do not lead others who are blind; the sighted do. Because of its obscurity, it can be applied to any number of situations. Matthew applies it to the Pharisees, and explains that the Pharisees are "blind guides" who are misleading the people (cf. Matt 23:13, 16, 24). Luke lists it in a series of sayings, describes it as a "parable," and explains it as a pupil's relation to a teacher (Luke 6:39–40). The saying appears in the *Ep. Apost.* 47 (middle second century), where it is applied to two persons, one of whom encourages another in sinning.

In *Thomas* the saying likely relates to the special character of the message brought by the living Jesus, to which the masses are blind (saying 28). All other religious leaders are impaired in their spiritual understanding and simply do not have the knowledge to lead people to the truth (saying 3a), or they know the truth but deliberately prevent others from finding it (sayings 39a and 102). In other words, *Thomas* is as sectarian in its religious views as were other leaders of the early Jesus movements (1 Cor 11:19; 2 Cor 11:1–15; Gal 1:6–9; 2:11–21; 2 Thess 2:1–5; 2 Tim 1:15; 2:16–18; Tit 3:10–11; 2 Pet 2:1; *Did.* 8:1–2; 11:1–2; *Barn.* 8:7; 9:4). See also saying 39a.

SAYING 35

No one can enter the house of the strong and take it by violence unless his hands are bound. Then the house may be plundered.

COMMENT

"It" can either be the house or the strong person. Compare saying 21b. The canonical parallels to this saying are Mark 3:27 = Matt 12:29 = Luke 11:21–22. Mark describes the saying as a "parable," meaning that for Mark it is allegory (see saying 9). Neither Matthew nor Luke calls it a parable, but in their narratives (Matt 12:22–30 = Mark 3:22–27 = Luke 11:14–23) the saying is treated allegorically, and the reader is forced to the following interpretation: Jesus is the strong man who enters Satan's domain and incapacitates him ("binds his hands"), and the proof of the plundering of Satan's domain is the casting out of demons.

In keeping with saying 1, however, *Thomas* does not have a helpful narrative context and does not provide explanations for sayings (see saying 21b) or provide clues leading toward a Thomasine explanation. A reading like Mark's (where the saying images a cosmic clash between God and a personified force of evil) seems unlikely as a Thomasine reading, however. *Thomas* is more like John in seeing the disciple as being involved in an ethical clash between the domain of darkness (the world) and the imperial rule of God. Both John and *Thomas* recognize that the earth or physical world may end (*Gos. Thom.* 11a and 111; John 6:39–40, 44 ["raise him at the last day" is a vestige of an apocalyptic expectation in John]), but in *Thomas* that ending is not explained as the conclusion of a cosmic drama. The struggle is in the spiritual arena (*Gos. Thom.* 22, 46, 49, 51, 108, and 113; John 3:17–19). In *Thomas* this saying is more likely a warning to the children of the living Father that even the spiritually enlightened (i.e., the strong) are at risk in the world (saying 21c). Among the early followers of Jesus, the "strong" (Rom 15:1; 1 Cor 4:10, 16:13) are those strong in faith (Rom 4:20), in the Lord (Eph 6:10–17), in the spirit (Gal 6:1), in grace (2 Tim 2:1); and even the stronger members of the community are always at risk in the world (Matt 24:24; 2 Tim 2:22–26; Gal 6:1; *Teach. Silv.* 85:1—86:23). Cf. Clement (*Exc.* 52.1; Stroker, *Extracanonical*

Unlocking the Secrets of the *Gospel according to Thomas*

Sayings, 138), who, like Thomas, also does not follow Mark's reading of the saying. For another take on the themes in the saying, see Pseudo-Clementine *Recogn.* 2.60.

SAYING 36

From dawn till dusk, or evening till morning, don't be anxious about what you will wear.

COMMENT

This brief saying is included in the mostly fragmentary and longer Greek version of the saying (Layton, *Nag Hammadi*, 121–22, 127). *Thomas* has only one focus of concern: what will be worn; but the Greek fragment is more extensive in focus: "food and what you will eat, and clothing and what you will wear." The Q tradition (Matt 6:25–34 = Luke 12:22–31) lacks the time reference appearing in *Thomas* ("dawn till dusk"; "evening till morning") and has more foci of concerns ("life," "eat" [Matthew adds, "and drink"], "body," "wear"). *Thomas*'s time reference indicates a twenty-four-hour period, suggesting that not one second of each day or evening should focus on anxieties about life's physical necessities (compare saying 14b: "eat what they set before you"). Saying 11b poses the issue of what is significant for life: does one focus on physical or spiritual concerns? Saying 36 completely dismisses the importance of physical concerns. The early Jesus communities domesticated this radical vision (1 Tim 6:7–8; *Did.* 12:3–4; 13.1–7) by pooling resources to care for the needs of others (Acts 2:44–45; 1 Cor 16:1–4; Rom 15:25–29; 2 Cor 8–9; Gal 2:10; Phil 4:15–18; *Did.* 4:8; *Gos. Thom.* 69b), by developing a social ministry for the needy of the community (1 Tim 5:9–16), and by making care for others a concern of the individual followers of Jesus (Jas 1:27; 2:15–16). Nevertheless, glimmerings of the original vision of Jesus (Matt 6:11 = Luke 11:13) survived, although it is not pervasive in the communities (Phil 4:11–12, 19). *Thomas* has preserved the original, radical vision of Jesus in this saying.

SAYING 37

His disciples asked, "When will you be revealed to us, and when will we see you?"

Jesus replied, "When you divest yourselves of shame, take your garments and put them beneath your feet like little children, and tread on them, [then you will see] the son of the One-Who-Lives and not be afraid.

COMMENT

The Greek parallel is fragmentary (Layton, *Nag Hammadi*, 122, 128) but clearly reads, "when you disrobe and are not ashamed" instead of, as in *Thomas*, "when you divest yourselves of shame." The disciples' questions are odd. Obviously they can "see" Jesus, because they are talking to him (see saying 24), but they want to "see" him revealed as his true self. Now he appears in human form (Phil 2:5–8), but the disciples are portrayed as thinking that there was more to him than that (in saying 28 the living Jesus appears "in flesh"). In *Gos. Sav.* 107:1–30, the disciples ask a similar question: "O Lord, in what form will you reveal yourself to us, or in what kind of body will you come?" And they add, "when you come to reveal yourself to us in all your glory" . . . "lest we see you and despair from fear." Because of their faith, the early Jesus communities believed that Jesus would appear differently in the future (for example, Mark 9:2–8 = Matt 17:1–8 = Luke 9:28–36; John 1:14; 17:5, 24; Phil 2:9–11; *Gos. Judas* 35:7–25; 2 Pet 1:16–19; Rev 1:7, 9–18); they had never seen him "as he is" (1 John 3:2; Heb 2:8–9). Jesus tells the disciples how they can see him as his true self (cf. saying 91). They can "see" him only through the eyes of innocence. The writer of Hebrews puts it differently: without holiness no one will see the Lord (12:14). Paul and the Pauline school use different language, yet the sentiment is the same: they must divest themselves of the old and put on the new (Eph 4:22–24; Col 3:9–10; cf. 2 Cor 5:17). In *Thomas*, in order to see Jesus as he is, one must, as a child (saying 22), regain the innocence of Eden.

Being "clothed with shame" is a Semitic idiom (Job 8:22; Ps 35:26; 89:45; 132:18; 1 Macc 1:28). Nakedness is also associated with shame (Mic 1:11; Jer 13:26; Jdt 9:2; Rev 3:18). In *Thomas* the disciples are to strip themselves of "shame" (symbolized by the garments they wear) and become like innocent children (for "innocent children" see 2 Macc 8:4). The images used in Jesus's answer evoke the fall of Adam and Eve from a state of innocence in Eden (Gen 2:25) to one of shame before God because of their nakedness (Gen 3:7, 10). Achieving the ideal state of the first human in Eden is a repeated theme in *Thomas* (sayings 22, 46, and 114). The saying may reflect early Christian baptismal practices. Even Paul associated the shift from old to new with baptism (Rom 6:3–4). "Stripping off garments" (see Dion. Ar. [fifth century] *e. h.* 396b–d), the person has all clothing removed for baptism, and after baptism is given new clothing (404c, 536b). Other parallels associating the saying with baptism are *Gos. Phil.* 75:21–25; Cyr. H. *catech. myst.* 20.2. For "trampling on the garment of shame," see the Greek *Gos. Eg.* (Schneemelcher and Wilson, *New Testament Apocrypha*, 1:211). Some interpret the stripping off of the garment of shame as the removal of the fleshly body (for example, DeConick, *Original Gospel of Thomas*, 153–54).

For "the One-Who-Lives" or "the living Father," see saying 50; the origin of the appellation "living" or "alive" is unclear. In the canonical tradition, the God of Israelite and Christian faith is called the "living God" (Ps 42:2; 84:2; Isa 37:4, 17; Jer 10:10). The expression is explained in several ways: God is the living God because he is the true God (Jer 10:10), because he is eternal (Dan 6:26), because he is the Creator (Acts 14:15), because he "lives" and idols do not (2 Cor 6:16; 1 Thess 1:9). For the image of stripping off clothes, see *Gos. Thom.* 21a.

Unlocking the Secrets of the *Gospel according to Thomas*

SAYING 38

You often wanted to hear these words I am speaking to you,
  and there was no other from whom to hear them.
There will be days when you seek me;
  you will not find me.

COMMENT

It is unclear who is addressed (as "you") in this saying. The address may be to the general public (as in saying 28) rather than special instruction to the "disciples" (as in saying 37), but one cannot be certain. A parallel to the saying attributed to a Latin *Book of Baruch* is cited in Cyprian of Carthage (third century) in *Treatise XII: Test.* 3:29 (see Stroker, *Extracanonical Sayings*, 191), and it is attributed to Lady Wisdom in Prov 1:28. Similar sayings are attributed to Jesus in the canonical tradition (Matt 13:17 = Luke 10:24; Luke 17:22; John 7:33–34); for other parallels see DeConick, *Original Gospel of Thomas*, 154–56. See *Thomas* sayings 92 and 59. The parallel in the Greek fragment (Layton, *Nag Hammadi*, 122–23, 128) is too fragmentary to read, and it is restored as the Coptic version. One finds a similar elitism or exclusiveness about their religious message among the earlier Jesus followers (Matt 13:35; Luke 10:21; John 6:66–69; Rom 8:19; 16:25–27; Eph 3:4–6, 8–10; 1 Pet 1:3–5, 12, 20).

Gospel of Thomas 38 is much more final than the canonical tradition about the "absence" of Jesus. In *Thomas*, when that time comes, Jesus will not be found. (Some translators add *and* after "when you seek me," which has the effect of softening the statement.) In the canonical tradition, when Jesus is absent (John 8:21; 13:33; 14:19; 16:16–19), he leaves a surrogate, the Holy Spirit (John14:16–19, 25–26; 20:22). The Spirit or Holy Spirit is largely absent from *Thomas* (see sayings 29, 44, 53, and 114), and its role, if it has any, is not addressed. In *Thomas* the living Jesus continues to be present in his words, so it is surprising to hear him say that he will not be found.

SAYING 39A

The Pharisees and scribes have taken the keys of knowledge and hidden them. They neither entered nor did they permit those who wished to enter.

COMMENT

The Greek fragment (Layton, *Nag Hammadi*, 123, 128) is restored on the basis of the Coptic saying, which is a variation of a saying found in Q (Matt 23:13 = Luke 11:52). There are differences, however, between the canonical tradition and *Thomas*. In Matthew, the scribes and Pharisees shut up the imperial rule of heaven; and in Luke, the "lawyers" have taken away the key (singular) of knowledge. In Matthew, Peter is given the keys of the imperial rule of heaven (Matt 16:19).

Apparently the thrust of the saying in *Thomas* is that the Pharisees and scribes have not even used the keys to open the doors leading to knowledge for themselves, and, what is worse, they have prevented others from entering (probably into the imperial rule; saying 102 has a similar motif). In Jesus's day the Pharisees and the scribes were the authoritative teachers of Torah: "they sat on Moses's seat" (Matt 23:2–3) but had failed in their responsibility (Matt 23:13). Their specific identity in *Thomas*'s day is unclear, but likely they were close competitors who shared a similar outlook as the collector of *Thomas*, since they have what *Thomas* considers the "keys of knowledge," though they choose not to use them. The term "Pharisee" is used metaphorically by the author of the (second- or third-century) *Testim. Truth* 29:6–26. They are described as those who only hear with physical ears, rather than with the heart (or mind), and who are under the control of the demonic archons.

Along with sayings 25, 26, 88, 93, and 99, this saying suggests an in-group mentality and thereby evokes an outsider, competitor group. A strong Jewish community existed in Alexandria from the earliest period after the founding of the city. See *Gos. Thom.* 102, which expresses the same sentiment about the Pharisees as saying 39a.

Unlocking the Secrets of the *Gospel according to Thomas*

SAYING 39B

But you become shrewd as snakes and simple as pigeons.

COMMENT

The saying is known in Matt 10:16b, where it is tied to the commissioning of the twelve disciples. Originally it would have been an independent saying that Matthew tied to the context of the commissioning with "therefore" or "so." Here Thomas has tied it to 39a with "but," to form a contrast to the irresponsibility of the scribes and Pharisees. In form, the saying is a paradox. It is impossible to be both shrewd and simple at the same time (see the discussion in Hedrick, *Many Things in Parables*, vii–ix). The word "simple" carries the idea of being uncomplicated or guileless, rather than stupid. Thus Jesus's followers are to be both shrewd and simple with respect to the "keys of knowledge." They are to handle the keys rightly (cf. 2 Tim 2:15). Shrewdness and lack of duplicity are called for with respect to the "keys." Followers of Jesus are to make the "keys of knowledge" available (saying 33a) to those who seek them (saying 62a). Saying 39b is used in *Teach. Silv.* 95:7–11; Ignatius *Pol.* 2:2; and Clement *Strom.* 7.82.6–7 to describe the expected character of the thoroughly equipped religious person.

SAYING 40

A grapevine was planted apart from the Father, and since it was not firmly set, it will be pulled up by its root and die.

COMMENT

This obscure saying, unknown in the canonical tradition, raises more questions than it answers. Who planted the grapevine? Who will pull it up by its roots? What exactly does "being planted apart from" (literally: "outside of") the Father denote? Some scholars have sensed that something is missing from the text and have supplied words to complete the thought: Patterson, Robinson, and Bethge have in *Fifth Gospel*, 17: "a grapevine was planted outside (the vineyard) of the Father"; DeConick, *Original Gospel of Thomas*, 161, has: "a grapevine has been planted apart from the Father's (planting)." Read against parallels in the Christian tradition that focus on God as the true planter of faith (Matt 15:13; *Gos. Phil.* 85:29–31; Isa 60:21; Herm. *Sim.* 5.5.2 and 5.6.2; cf. John 15:5–6; Isa 5:1–7; see other parallels in DeConick, *Original Gospel of Thomas*, 161–62), this saying invalidates all other competitive plantings. In this context the competitors of sayings 39a and 39b are evoked. Pulling up a tree or vine by its root is the proper way to eliminate it (but cf. Matt 3:10 = Luke 3:9). If it is cut down (cf. Luke 13:7), the root will only sprout again. So the saying envisions a time when the "competitors" will be utterly destroyed.

SAYING 41

Whoever has will receive, and whoever has not, even the little they do have will be taken away.

COMMENT

This cryptic saying is also known in the canonical tradition. It appears as a Markan saying (4:25), which is slightly revised by Matthew (13:12) and Luke (8:18) and used in different literary contexts, which help to clarify the saying as each evangelist understands it. In each of these cases what is possessed, or not possessed, is knowledge of the secrets of the imperial rule. In Q (Matt 25:29 = Luke 19:26), at issue are the rewards given to servants for their faithful handling of the talents/pounds: those who wisely invest what they have will receive more; those who do not invest lose what they have. In the *Apoc. Pet.* 83:15—84:6, the saying contrasts the state of the one possessing immortality and the state of those who belong to the mortal realm. In each case the literary context of the saying provides the meaning of what is possessed and lost. In *Thomas* there is no narrative context to suggest what is possessed or lost (but cf. saying 60).

The saying is a proverb (Bultmann, *History of the Synoptic Tradition*, 108; Dalman, *Jesus-Jeshua*, 228) on "having and not having," and appears elsewhere in the ancient world, particularly in rabbinic literature (see *4 Ezra* 7:25; *Gos. Phil.* 76:17–22; and the rabbinic parallels to Matt 13:12 in Strack and Billerbeck, *Kommentar* 1:660–62). In *Thomas* the saying may be read in connection with the Pharisees and scribes (so DeConick, *Original Gospel of Thomas*, 162), with the competitor group so designated as "scribes and Pharisees" (cf. sayings 39a, 39b, and 40), or more broadly, as related to whatever is possessed by the radical follower of Jesus (so Valantasis, *Gospel of Thomas*, 117) but not possessed by others (see 3b and 70).

SAYING 42

Come into being as you pass away.

COMMENT

The popular translation of this saying is "become passers by." In this form the saying is generally understood as encouraging a disengagement from the world. See DeConick, *Original Gospel of Thomas*, 164, for a summary of other ways the saying has been translated and understood. The Coptic saying uses a Greek loanword (παράγειν) to express "pass." In the canonical gospels this Greek word when used in the absolute (i.e., by itself with nothing added to it) means simply "pass" (Matt 20:30; Mark 2:14; 15:21). English translators may sometimes add an additional English word such as *on* to make the word "pass" when used alone sound better to the English ear; hence it is translated as "pass on," as in the examples above. In Greek, on the other hand, additional words or expressions are frequently added to the word (cf. Matt 9:9, 27; Ps 143:4 LXX). In the *Gospel of Thomas* this Greek word also appears in saying 11a in the absolute, with the obvious meaning in English idiom of "passing away" or "disappearing." It is also used this way in the New Testament and is rendered "pass" or "pass away" (1 Cor 7:31; 1 John 2:8, 17). In Coptic, the Greek loanword is used and then translated with certain English expressions to complete it (*Disc. 8–9*, 62:19–20; *Treat. Seth*, 56:28; 58:10; *Testim. Truth* [30:16]; *Dial. Sav*.124:3; *Bala'izah* 187:3; 32:102). Hence "pass" or "pass away" seems a better rendering for the Coptic than "passersby." But compare the translation of a circumstantial participle as an attributive participle ("passerby," Mark 15:21) to solve the awkward problem of double circumstantial participles modifying "Simon."

A similar conceptual parallel to the translation of saying 42 appears in the New Testament: "though our outer nature is wasting away, our inner nature is being renewed" (2 Cor 4:16; cf. Luke 9:23–24; John 12:24–25; Rom 6:6–9; 1 Cor 15:36–38, 42–45; 2 Cor 5:17; Eph 4:22–24; Col 3:9–10). A similar idea to "become by passing away" appears in the later Christian tradition: "Die that you may live" (*Acts John* 76 [third century]: Schneemelcher and Wilson, *New Testament Apocrypha* 2:198). In the Hermetic tradition, as the awareness of the body passes away, the individual enters into God (*Corp. herm.* 1.24–26: Copenhaver, *Hermetica*, 5–6): "The human rises up to heaven . . . he comes to be on high without leaving the earth behind" (*Corp. herm.* 10.25: Copenhaver, *Hermetica*, 36). See also the description of the Peratae in Hippolytus *Ref.* 5.16.1: "coming into being by certain routes to cross over destruction." In the literature cited above, the concept of "coming to be as you pass away" is understood three different ways: on a cosmic model (i.e., dying: Rom 6:6–9; 1 Cor 15:36–38, 42–45; Hippolytus *Ref.* 5.16.1); on an ethical model (i.e., lifestyle: John 12:24–25; 2 Cor 5:17; Eph 4:22–24; Col 3:9–10); on a psychological model (i.e., the character of the inner person: 2 Cor 4:16; *Corp. herm.* 1.24–26; Plotinus *Enn.* VI, 9, 8–11). The collector of the *Gospel of Thomas* would likely have understood the paradoxical saying psychologically, as an inner mystical ascent into the divine (see sayings 3b and 11c on mystical union with the divine).

SAYING 43

His disciples said to him, "Who are you to tell us these things?"
"Do you not know who I am from what I tell you? You certainly have become like the Jews. For they hate the tree and love the fruit, and love the fruit yet hate the tree."

COMMENT

The temptation is to read sayings 42 and 43 as one saying. Jesus makes a statement (42), and the disciples follow it with a question (43). Only one other dialogue, however, begins with a statement by Jesus followed by questions from the disciples (22). Saying 61, sometimes regarded as another instance of a statement followed by a question, actually appears to be two independent sayings: 61a and 61b. Saying 61a is a statement by Jesus, unrelated to 61b, while 61b begins with a question by Salome and is followed by a response from Jesus. This form appears frequently in *Thomas* (see sayings 6a, 21a, 37, 43, 51, 53, and 113); other sayings begin with a statement to Jesus, followed by a saying of Jesus (see sayings 12, 18, 20, 24, 52, 72, 79a, 91, 99, 100, 104, and 114). Reading sayings 42 and 43 as two independent sayings, however, leaves in question what it was Jesus said to the disciples prompting their original question. But on the other hand, reading them as one saying turns the answer to the disciples' question in 43 into a nonanswer, for in that case Jesus does not give a direct answer to their question. Reading 42 and 43 independently forces the reader to understand "these things" about which the disciples ask as all the sayings in *Thomas*.

Here in saying 43 Jesus expresses surprise at the disciples' inability to understand his sayings. (See saying 91 for a similar unperceptive statement by an interlocutor of Jesus.) This happens frequently in this text (see saying 22). Whether the term "Jew" is intended to evoke an ethnic group or is an epithet of abuse (similar to the situation in sayings 39a and 102) derogating the competitors of the collector of these sayings is unclear. But the contrast between disciples and Jews situates the saying at the end of the first century at the earliest (cf. the situation in the Gospel of John, where the opponents of Jesus are "the Jews," i.e., Judeans). The term "Jew" could be a social code since there were extensive Jewish communities in Egypt from a very early period (see the Introduction).

It is clear, however, that this group has a divided opinion regarding the tree and its fruit. Some interpreters have cited New Testament parallels (Luke 6:43–44; Matt 7:16–20; 12:33) and explain the saying as an allegory on a tree and its fruit alluding to types of human behavior. But possibly the reference is to a particular tree, and the disagreements concern the tree of the knowledge of good and evil (Gen 3:1–22). Being able to know the difference between good and evil is always a good thing in principle (Amos 5:11–15; Mic 3:1–4). In some radical Christian (Gnostic) groups, the Garden of Eden story was interpreted positively as an escape from the tyranny of the Demiurge through the acquisition of *gnosis* (knowledge), for the acquisition made one like God: to know the difference between good and evil (Gen 3:5, 22; see *Orig. World*, NHC II,5:118:24—119:18). In rabbinic traditions, on the other hand, after Adam ate the fruit, wisdom departed from him, and he experienced lust and desire (Gen 4:1). The tree of the knowledge of good and evil is even called the tree of desire and lust (see Ginzberg, *Legends of the Jews*, 1:69–83, 90). Hence Adam lost wisdom but gained carnal knowledge; but in radical Christian texts Adam gained true spiritual insight. In the same way Jesus's disciples are chided in *Thomas* for having mixed ideas about Jesus's identity (see saying 13).

SAYING 44

Whoever blasphemes the Father will be forgiven, and whoever blasphemes the son will be forgiven; but whoever blasphemes the Holy Spirit will not be forgiven—neither on earth nor in heaven.

COMMENT

This saying has two partial parallels in the Synoptic Gospels, Mark (3:28–29) and Q (Matt 12:31–32; Luke 12:10). All three Synoptic Gospels omit "blasphemy against the Father," and only Matthew parallels *Thomas*'s ending by adding "either in this age or the age to come." Q adds "blasphemy against the Son of Man." It is surprising to find mention in *Thomas* of the "Holy Spirit," which plays such a significant role in the New Testament, but not in *Thomas*. *Thomas* regularly refers to the spiritual nature of the human being (sayings 14a, 53, 29), which may become a living spirit (114), but no practical role for a Holy Spirit (see saying 38) is found in the collection of sayings in *Thomas*. Aside from this unexpected mention of the Holy Spirit in saying 44, there is no surrogate for the divine presence as there is, for example, in the Gospel of John (14:18–19, 25–26; 15:26).

Jesus in *Thomas* is always present in his words, which bring immortality (saying 1), and the Father is immediately present to the inner person (saying 3b). For "the Father," see sayings 15, 27, 40, 50, 57, 64b, 69a, 79a, 83, 96, 98, 99, and 113; for the "living Father," see sayings 3b and 50; for the "One-Who-Lives," see sayings 37, 59, and 111. The terms "Father" and "living Father" are apparently interchangeable (saying 50). The bare term *son* as a designation for Jesus does not appear elsewhere in *Thomas*; the "*son* of the One-Who-Lives" appears once (saying 37), and the term "son of man" appears once (saying 86), where it is translated "Adam's child." The apparent Trinitarian formula—Father, Son, and Holy Spirit—is a standard confession in orthodox theology, but there is no Trinitarian dogma in *Thomas* (see Matt 28:19, where a similar saying appears without a developed concept of the Trinity in the document as a whole). Saying 44 is evidence of *Thomas*'s continued adaptation to its social context and a reminder that although *Thomas* is likely an early text (perhaps even first-century), it had a long, adaptable life, certainly well past the rise of orthodoxy in the mid-fourth century.

SAYING 45A

A grape is not harvested from a thorn tree, nor is a fig gathered from a thistle plant, for they don't bear fruit.

COMMENT

This proverb has a close parallel to a Q tradition (Matt 7:16 = Luke 6:43). The saying appeals to popular wisdom—that is, to common sense (compare Jas 3:11–12); the incongruity of fruit being derived from thorns and thistles is striking, and serves as a setup for saying 45b, which serves as an explanation of the proverb in 45a. Matthew applies the proverb to the identification of false prophets who pretend to be something they are not (Matt 7:15); Luke more generally applies the proverb to the lives of "good" and "evil" men (Luke 6:45), which is also how it seems *Thomas* understands the proverb.

SAYING 45B

From a treasure trove a good person brings forth good;
  from an evil hoard in the heart a bad person brings forth evil and
    speaks evil—
  for from the abundance of the heart comes forth evil.

COMMENT

The saying has a Q parallel (Matt 12:35 = Luke 6:45). In Coptic the words for "treasure trove" and "hoard" are the same, but the present translation derives from the sharp contrast between the good person and the bad person. These centers in the human heart described as "treasure" (cf. Matt 6:21) are clearly not the same, for one produces good and the other evil: hence the translation "hoard," which has a slightly negative connotation. The storehouse from which both good and evil come lies in the heart, although *Thomas* does not specifically affirm this for the good person (i.e., "in the heart" is not stated); compare Luke, where the heart as the source of virtue or vice is affirmed for the good person but not the bad person (6:45).

The *Thomas* saying, like its Q parallel, forms a balanced, antithetical parallel; although the *Thomas* saying adds that the bad person "speaks evil (Matt 12:36–37), which is implied by the conclusion in *Thomas*. *Thomas*'s conclusion ("for from the abundance of the heart comes forth evil") also concludes Luke's version of the saying (6:45b), but in Matthew (12:34b) it introduces the saying. The idea of behavior arising from within the inner person is well known in the Jewish and Christian traditions (Sir 27:6; Mark 7:20–23 = Matt 15:18–20) and *Thomas* (14c). For other parallels, see DeConick, *Original Gospel of Thomas*, 167–68.

SAYING 46

Among those born of women from Adam to John the Baptizer, no one is more exalted than John, lest his eyes be downcast. But I have said, whoever among you becomes a child will know the imperial rule and be higher than John.

COMMENT

John the Baptizer is accorded a lofty position in the canonical tradition (Q: Luke 7:28 = Matt 11:11), where he is known as the forerunner of the Messiah believed to be prophesied in Jewish Scripture (Luke 7:24–27 = Matt 11:7–10). And now in *Thomas*, John is accorded the status of "none greater than he." *Thomas* does not say why John is described as the most exalted human being since Adam (for Adam, see saying 85), but since Jesus is not known as Messiah in *Thomas*, there must be another reason for Jesus to praise John. John's exalted status, however, is surpassed by a "child," i.e., an enlightened follower of Jesus (see the discussion of sayings 22, 4a, 15, 21a), who by virtue of experiencing God's imperial rule will achieve a higher status than John, for the children of God's imperial rule are not "born of woman" but born of God (saying 50: "We are his sons and the elect of the living Father"; cf. John 1:12–13; 3:3–8; 1 John 2:29; 4:7). "Lest his eyes be downcast," i.e., show deference to another (cf. Prov 30:13; Isa 5:15). The periodizing of time using John as a transition point is also known in Matt 11:12–14 (but cf. Luke 16:16), where Matthew includes John in the new period of the proclamation of the imperial rule of God.

SAYING 47A

*No one can mount two horses
   or draw two bows;
and it is impossible for a servant to submit to two masters—
   or else one will be held in honor and the other treated shamefully.*

COMMENT

Saying 47 is composed of a string of independent proverbs. A proverb is the distillation of community wisdom (common sense) whose sense is immediately obvious at a literal level, but whose specific meaning must be derived from the context to which the proverb is applied. This first proverb (saying 47a) consists of two parallel strands. The first strand is unattested as a saying of Jesus; the second strand, followed by an explanation made up of a single strand, is a Q tradition (Luke 16:13a = Matt 6:24a). The explanation (Luke 16:13b = Matt 6:24b) consists of two parallel strands ("hate one . . . love the other"; "devoted to one . . . despise the other"), neither of which agrees with *Thomas* ("honor . . . treat shamefully"). The first strand of *Thomas* 47a describes physical impossibilities, and the second relates to divided loyalties. As it is not possible to perform certain physical acts, just so it is not possible to render complete loyalty to two primary commitments at the same time, which is exactly the way Q understood primary commitment: "You cannot serve God and mammon" (Luke 16:13c = Matt 6:24c). *Thomas* expresses similar sentiments about primary commitments in sayings 55 and 101 (see sayings 47b, 47c, and 47d).

Unlocking the Secrets of the *Gospel according to Thomas*

SAYING 47B

No one drinks aged wine and instantly wants young wine to drink.

COMMENT

Saying 47b appears in Luke as a conclusion (Luke 5:39) to a proverb about wine packaging (Luke 5:37–38). *Thomas*, however, employs the saying to introduce a similar statement about wine packaging. Luke's conclusion (5:39) places greater value on wine that is aged than on young (or new) wine, which is not quite ready to drink. Of course some wines are consumed when young, but Luke's conclusion (5:39) looks at the general rule that aged wines are better, cf. Sir 9:10; not all wine is of the same quality, cf. Acts 2:13; John 2:9–10; Sir 31:28; 32:6; Pliny *Nat. Hist.* 14.4.21; 14.4.31–32. The proverb in Luke (5:37–38) describes the packaging of new wine, while Luke's conclusion stresses an exclusive preference for aged wines over young wines. *Thomas*, on the other hand, holds out the possibility that some may drink new wine, but just not after drinking aged wine. At the precise moment of drinking aged wine (i.e., "instantly"), they may not want new wine, but may at another time drink it. In other words, *Thomas* is playing off against the conventional view of wines and thereby turns proverb into metaphor. *Thomas* is not talking about wine at all, but rather about a new "gospel" (saying 33a). In terms of the metaphor, the gospel is a new wine that will open minds intoxicated by the commonly preferred aged wines (saying 28)—that is, conventional wisdom (see sayings 47a, 47c, and 47d).

SAYING 47C

New wine is not put into an old wineskin
  lest it burst,
and aged wine is not put into a new wineskin
  lest the skin ruin the wine.

COMMENT

The parallel in the Synoptic Gospels (Matt 9:17 = Mark 2:22 = Luke 5:37–38) describes the process of packaging new wine and the use of wineskins. Because new wine ferments (Job 32:18–19 LXX; during fermentation it is either must or sweet wine), it will destroy the skin if placed in an old wineskin; therefore new wine is placed in fresh skins to allow room for expansion. *Thomas*, on the other hand, contrasts the packaging of young and aged wine. The rule is, new wine is for new skins and aged wine for old skins. The reason is, new wine ruins old skins, and new skins ruin the taste of already aged wine. In terms of the metaphor of 47b, the new wine of *Thomas*'s gospel requires new forms (see sayings 14a, 47a, 47b, and 47d). On the use of wineskins, see McGovern et al., *Origin and Ancient History of Wine*, 115–16, 118–19, 252; and Immerwahr, "New Wine in Ancient Wineskins," particularly 128–31).

SAYING 47D

An old patch is not sewn onto a new garment since a tear would result.

COMMENT

This saying is a shorter form of a saying known in the Synoptic Gospels (Mark 2:21 = Matt 9:16 = Luke 5:36), which consists of a brief principle (Mark 2:21a = Matt 9:16a = Luke 5:36a) followed by an explanation (Mark 2:21b = Matt 9:16b = Luke 5:36b). Note that Luke's explanation for why one does not use new cloth on an old garment (i.e., one not only tears a new garment, but the piece from the new garment will not match the old) differs from Matthew and Mark (i.e., the patch tears away from the old garment and makes the tear worse). In *Thomas*, however, old patches are not put on new garments, because there would be a tear (so *Thomas* agrees with Mark and Matthew). What *Thomas* conceives as tearing is unclear, however: is the patch or the garment torn, or does the patch pull away from the garment? In one sense it does not really matter what is torn, because the integrity of the old garment is damaged in each case. In terms of the metaphor, the result is the same: the old ways are not appropriate to accommodate the new gospel (see sayings 14a; 47a, 47b, and 47c).

SAYING 48

If two make peace with one another in this single household, they will say to the mountain, "Go away," and it will move.

COMMENT

In general, the saying celebrates the spiritual force of reconciliation and harmony: nothing is impossible to those united in singleness of purpose. A similar idea is expressed in saying 106. On singularity and unity, see saying 4b. The spiritual force is not a power that belongs to just anyone, but it is to "this single [i.e., particular] household" that the power belongs. Although the focused group is unstated, likely a *Thomas* community is intended (see sayings 25, 26, 39a, 39b, and 40 on community). The real question is the nature of the saying. Is this literal language, and hence "magic" (see saying 19b), or is it hyperbole? The New Testament parallels (Matt 18:19; 17:20; Matt 21:21–22 = Mark 11:21–24; Luke 17:6; 1 Cor 13:2) to the saying raise the same question. It is a very difficult question to answer since hyperbole is easily understood literally. The closest parallel to saying 48 is a saying with this same combination of making peace with one another (cf. Matt 18:19) and moving a mountain (cf. Matt 17:20) appearing in a third-century church order (the Syrian *Didasc. Apost.* 15:25: Connolly, *Didascalia Apostolorum*, 134): "for it is written in the Gospel: 'If two shall agree together, and shall ask anything whatsoever, it shall be given them. And if they shall say to a mountain that it be removed and fall into the sea, it shall so be done.'"

Unlocking the Secrets of the *Gospel according to Thomas*

SAYING 49

The solitary and chosen are favored, for you will discover the imperial rule. Since you are from it, you will go there again.

COMMENT

On the identity of the solitary and chosen, see sayings 16b, 23, and 75 (the expression "elect and solitary" occurs in *Dial. Sav.* 120:26). On "favored," see saying 19a. On the idea of returning to the beginning, see saying 18. The reason that the solitary ones discover the imperial rule is that they have an innate inclination toward God's reign (saying 19a). It is an awareness of God owing to their pre-existent origins, and for this reason they are destined to return to the imperial rule. Many of the concepts in saying 49 were already available in the ancient world. For example, in the Jewish tradition, the preexistence of the soul (Wis 8:19–20); in the Christian tradition, God's foreknowledge of the child of God (Rom 8:29–30; 11:2) and the prior election or calling of the child of God (Mark 13:20; 1 Pet 1:1–2; 2 Pet 1:10; 2 Tim 1:8–9). In the Hermetic tradition, those who "are from light and life" will "advance there again" (*Corp. herm.* 1.21). The preexistence and immortality of the soul are best known from Platonic thought (see the discussion in the *Phaedo*), but the concepts were widespread throughout Graeco-Roman antiquity. In Valentinianism, followers of the Christian-Gnostic teacher Valentinus (second century) divided humankind into three categories: the pneumatics or spirituals, who were marked for salvation; the psychics, who could be saved through the church; and the hylics, who belonged to the material world (see Epiphanius *Pan.* 2.23.1, quoting Irenaeus). Valentinus referred to the spirituals as "the perfect" (*Gos. Truth* 18:11–21), and described them as those who emanated from the Father (*Gos. Truth* 21:18–25), because they had been called in the foreknowledge of the Father (*Gos. Truth* 21:25–30). Paul uses similar descriptions—the spirituals (1 Cor 2:15—3:1) and the psychics (1 Cor 2:14)—and describes Adam as *choicos* (χοϊκός), a man of dust (1 Cor 15:47–48; cf. Gen 2:7). The *Gospel of Thomas* shares affinities with this way of thinking by partitioning humanity into three "classes": the solitary, the disciples, and "humanity's children" (see sayings 22 and 24 for the disciples, and saying 28 for humanity's children).

SAYING 50

If you are asked, "Where have you come from?"
  Tell them, "We have come from the source of the self-generated light—the light emerged and appeared in their image."
If you are asked, "Is it you?"
  Tell them, "We are its [i.e., the light's] children; we are the chosen of the living Father."
If you are asked, "What is the sign of your Father who is in you?"
  Tell them, "Motion and repose."

COMMENT

The saying in form resembles a catechesis or a litany of confessions. Some suggest that a context for the "confessions" in saying 50 might be found in the ascent of the individual soul at death through the series of principalities and powers that seek to prohibit the soul's escape from the material world (Rom 8:38–39; Eph 6:12; Col 2:15). If the ascent of the soul is the proper context for the saying, the answers in saying 50 are designed to permit the soul to reach the next level in the ascent. Irenaeus lists three answers given by the ascending soul: "I am a child of the preexistent Father"; "I trace my origin from the preexistent Father"; "I am coming again to the place from whence I went forth" (Irenaeus *Haer.* 1.21.5). See also *1 Apoc. Jas.* 32:28—34:20 and *Apoc. Paul* 23:1—24:8, where similar questions and answers are found in a similar mythical context. But in the case of saying 50 it is unknown whether the interrogators are mythical or human, or whether the context is earthly or mythical.

It is possible that the responses are part of an early Christian ritual of some sort—for example, baptism. Some form of instruction preceded Christian baptism in the second century (Justin *1 Apol.* 61), and the *Didache* prior to baptism (7:1) incorporated certain instructions (1:1—6:3) for the initiate. Acts 8:37, while now considered a later addition to Acts, suggests that the confession of the Ethiopian eunuch in 8:37 was used by the church for baptismal ceremonies ("And Philip said, 'If you believe with all your heart, you may.' And he replied, 'I believe that Jesus Christ is the Son of God.'"). In the *Apostolic Constitutions* (third century) candidates for baptism were to "renounce Satan" and make certain affirmative confessions (7:40–41). The baptismal ceremonies described in Pseudo-Dionysus the Areopagite, *e. h.* 393A–397A (fifth and sixth centuries) included a segment where the hierarch asks why the initiate has come, and the initiate replies "in accordance with the instructions given him by his sponsor" (Luibheid, *Pseudo-Dionysus*, 202).

The individual answers in the *Thomas* litany, however, do have a striking similarity to the answers in Irenaeus, with respect to origin, identity, and destination. Response 1: We originate in the source of the self-generated Light. The light is an ethical, spiritual reality (saying 24), identified here (saying 50) and throughout the ancient world as a divine, spiritual order (see saying 24 for the contrast between light and darkness). It is also the inner essence of the children of the light—of those associated with the divine order (sayings 11b, 61b, 77a, 83). The "light" image is freely used in early Christianity: of God (Jas 1:17; 1 John 1:5; Rev 21:23); of the disciple (Matt 5:14; Luke 16:8; John 12:36; 1 Thess 5:5; Eph 5:8); of Jesus (John1:4–8; 8:12; 9:5); and of the divine world (1 Tim 6:16). The children of the light originate in the place of light and to it will return (sayings 18, 19a, and 49).

Response 2: We are the light's children and the chosen of the living Father (saying 23). The children of the light are the elect and chosen of the living Father in *Thomas* (sayings 3b and 49).

Response 3: The only sign offered for their identity is "motion and repose." For "repose," cf. sayings 51, 60, and 90; Matt 11:29. *Thomas* does not clarify "motion," as such; but see sayings 19, 48, 78, and 106. "Movement and rest" are simultaneous conditions of the Platonic "One," or "Unity" (for "One," see sayings 4b, 22, 23, and 106). Nevertheless, the One cannot be said to be in either motion or repose, for it both is and is not; see Allen, *Parmenides*, 335–36 (discussing *Parm.* 162B–163B). In Plotinus *Enn.* VI.9.3, "movement and rest" are states pertaining to Being. Compare the judgment of the Naassenes, who argued that the "being who moves everything does not move" (Hippolytus *Ref.* 5.7.25). From this perspective, the sign offered by the initiate in *Thomas* is the inner presence of the Father (saying 3b).

"Their image": the reference is unclear. Perhaps it is an oblique reference to the mythical idea that the creation of the first human (Adam) was an attempt by the powers of darkness to capture an image of a divine being left behind in the primordial waters. What they fabricated was lifeless until a divine spirit infused life into the creature (*Hyp. Arch.* 87:11—88:24). Or perhaps it alludes to the Father's light that has come to reside in human beings (see saying 83).

SAYING 51

His disciples asked him, "When will the repose of the dead occur, and when will the new world come?"
 He replied, "What you are looking for has come, but you don't recognize it."

COMMENT

This saying plays off against two popular beliefs about the end of all things, but which in this saying are conceived as one and the same event ("What" and "it" translate singular pronouns). In Semitic antiquity it was believed that the dead would attain "rest" (Sir 22:11; 30:17; 38:23), but the idea of the dead attaining rest was challenged by the idea of the renewal of the creation (Isa 65:17; 66:22; 2 Esd 2:34; Rom 8:19-21; Rev 21:1), which raised the question of the eventual rest of the dead (2 Esd 7:75). *Thomas* conceives these concepts in a spiritual sense (death: John 5:25; 11:25-26; 1 John 3:13-14; Eph 2:1, 5; new creation: 2 Cor 5:17). Both the repose of the dead and the coming of the new world have already occurred (cf. 2 Tim 2:16-18) spiritually in the experience of the solitary and elect (sayings 3b and 113; 16b, 49, 50, 75, 22).

SAYING 52

His disciples said to him, "Twenty-four prophets spoke in Israel, and they all spoke on your account."
　　He replied, "You have abandoned the One-Who-Lives, who is before you, and talked about those who are dead."

COMMENT

Twenty-four prophets likely refer to the twenty-four books of the Hebrew Bible (2 Esd 14:45), which were divided into three categories: law, prophets, and writings. These books are the same as the thirty-nine books in the Protestant Old Testament, only divided differently. The Septuagint and the Catholic Bible have a few more books included. Early Christians used the Septuagint rather than the Hebrew as their Holy or Sacred Scripture (Rom 1:2; 2 Tim 3:15), and they came to think of it as one collection—either the "Scripture" (Mark 15:28; John 7:38, 42; 1 Tim 5:18; 2 Tim 3:16; Gal 3:8, 22; Jas 2:23; 2 Pet 1:20), or the "Scriptures" (2 Pet 3:16). They regarded all parts as "prophetic utterance" in the sense that God was revealing Jesus the Christ in them (John 1:45; 5:39; Luke 24:27; Acts 18:28; Rom 16:26). Hence they read Scripture "prophetically" in the sense that what the Scriptures revealed went beyond the literal meaning of the words (for example, Matthew's interpretation of Isa 7:14 = Matt 1:20–23). Even in the Jewish tradition, Moses was considered a prophet (Philo *Mos.* 2.3.135; 2.35.187–88; Josephus *Ant.* 4.8.49; *Test. Moses* 11:16).

　　The disciples, as usual in *Thomas* (saying 22), lack understanding and are corrected: "Scripture" is not the authority; rather the authority is the presence of the living Father within (sayings 11c, 22, and 106). The term "the One-Who-Lives" is always reserved for the living Father in *Thomas* (prologue, sayings 3b, 37, 59, and 111). In an essay (*Leg.* 2.4.14) Augustine quoted a saying of Jesus paralleling the response to the disciples in saying 52: "You have dismissed the living One who is before you, and you tell stories about the dead." Augustine said that his opponent had taken the testimony "from some apocryphal writing." The argument in Augustine (fourth and fifth centuries) is the same as in *Thomas*: a debate over Old Testament prophecy (see Plisch, *Gospel of Thomas*, 134–35).

SAYING 53

His disciples asked him, "Is circumcision beneficial or not?"
He replied, "If it were beneficial, their father would generate circumcised children from their mother. True circumcision is a matter of the spirit, and it is completely beneficial."

COMMENT

Again the disciples ask a "dumb" question revealing their spiritual ignorance (cf. saying 22). Jesus's answer treats the question as almost laughably inappropriate—that is to say, obviously circumcision is not "necessary," for if it were, children would be born circumcised. This saying is an interesting twist on what was a serious issue in Christian communities in the first century. In Judaism, male circumcision was the sign of belonging to the covenant community (Gen 17:1–14; Exod 12:48; Lev 12:3). The physical act was also treated metaphorically, i.e. as "spiritual circumcision" (Deut 10:16; 30:6; Jer 4:4). In early Christian communities, because the earliest followers of Jesus were Jewish, circumcision was a problem for gentiles coming into a church comprised for the most part of Jews (Gal 2:1–13).

The issue was, why should these Gentiles not also have to be circumcised like the rest of the Jewish members? Gentile Christians rejected circumcision as essential to Christian faith. *Thomas* also takes this perspective: true circumcision is a matter of the spirit (Rom 2:25–29; 3:27–31; Gal 5:6; 6:15; 1 Cor 7:19; Phil 3:3). In general, *Thomas* rejects the necessity of ritual (sayings 6a and 14a). *Thomas*, however, does not clarify what "spiritual circumcision" means but would clearly agree with Paul that real circumcision is a matter of the heart (Rom 2:29 and *Gos. Thom.* 3b). Jesus's answer to the disciples' question is similar to an argument by Justin that if circumcision were necessary God would have made Adam circumcised (*Dial.* 19.3).

SAYING 54

The poor are favored, for yours is Heaven's imperial rule.

COMMENT

On "favored," see saying 19a. See saying 6a for "Heaven" as a circumlocution for God. Heaven's imperial rule is also in saying 20. *Thomas*'s saying is closer to Luke's version (6:20b) of the Q beatitude than to Matthew's version (5:3), but *Thomas* shares features with both versions of the saying in the canonical evangelists. Luke reads, "Blessed are you poor for yours is God's imperial rule." Matthew reads, "Blessed are the poor in spirit, for theirs is heaven's imperial rule." The saying seems out of place in *Thomas*, where poverty (sayings 3b and 29), lack (saying 67), emptiness (sayings 28 and 97), and hunger (saying 69b) are negative concepts; each of these emphasizes a "lack" that needs "filling" (see *Gos. Sav.* 5F: 19–32). In *Thomas* the poor are the spiritually unenlightened of the world (saying 3b). They are the ones to whom the living Jesus came (saying 28) and therefore are the subjects of the evangelism (saying 33a) of the Thomasine community (see saying 39a) and representative of the "spiritual" lack in the world. Heaven's imperial rule is "theirs," however, in the sense that the imperial rule is characterized by persons such as them. Most commentators, however, understand the poor in this saying in a positive sense as the materially impoverished (cf. Isa 61:1; Jas 2:1–7).

Unlocking the Secrets of the *Gospel according to Thomas*

SAYING 55

Whoever does not hate father and mother will be unable to be my disciple; whoever does not hate brothers and sisters and come to the cross as I did will not be worthy of me.

COMMENT

This difficult saying is parallel to a Q saying (Matt 10:37–38 = Luke 14:26–27; cf. Matt 16:24 = Mark 8:34 = Luke 9:23) and has saying 101 as its doublet. For other parallels to saying 55 see DeConick, *Original Gospel of Thomas*, 190–91. In *Thomas* it is a two-strand saying—strand 1: "hate father-mother". . . "not be my disciple," and strand 2: "hate brothers-sisters and come to the cross" . . . "not worthy of me." Luke, also two-stranded, is close to *Thomas* but still quite different—strand 1: "hate father, mother, wife, children, brothers, sisters, and own life" . . . "not be disciple"; and strand 2: "not bear own cross and come after me" . . . "not worthy of me." Matthew, a three-strand saying, is even more different—strand 1: "loves father, mother more" . . . "not worthy of me"; strand 2: "loves son, daughter more" . . . "not worthy of me"; and strand 3: "does not take up cross and follow" . . . "not worthy of me."

The saying is hyperbole (exaggeration for effect); Matthew's version states the issue literally: one who aspires to follow Jesus must be single minded in that pursuit. See saying 26 for another use of hyperbole in *Thomas*, and cf. Mark 9:42–48 for other hyperbolic language in the canonical tradition. For the fragmentation of the biological family unit caused by single-minded devotion to following Jesus, see *Thomas* sayings 16b, 99, 101, and 105 (and language reflective of single-minded devotion in Acts 20:22–25 and 1 Cor 9:16, 19–25). "Come to the cross as I did": most translators read, "take up the cross"; cf. attitudes toward the cross attributed to Jesus in Mark 14:32–42 and *Gos. Sav.* 99:3–18; 5H: 53–63. This *Thomas* saying has the only mention of Jesus's passion in *Thomas*: see the discussion in Plisch, *Gospel of Thomas*, 139. See also *Gos. Thom.* 105 on the biological family.

SAYING 56

Whoever has come to know the world has discovered a corpse, and the world is unworthy of anyone who has discovered a corpse.

COMMENT

In the second half of the saying, "anyone who has discovered a corpse" should likely be emended to read "anyone who has discovered <this> corpse," i.e., anyone discovering the world for what it really is. Saying 80 is a duplicate of saying 56, except that it reads "body" where saying 56 reads "corpse." For the negative view of "world" in *Thomas* and early Christianity, see the discussion at saying 21c, and cf. sayings 110 and 111. In Manichaeism the "worlds below" are described as body and carcass (*Kephalaia* chap. 48, pp. 120:31—121:2). Like the distinction between light and darkness (saying 24), the description of the world as corpse and body is metaphorical rather than literal. In short, the world is a "dead" place, a place bereft of life and light, and hence unworthy of anyone who has come to know the world for what it really is (cf. Heb 11:37–38). Coming to recognize the true state of the world is the equivalent of finding oneself (sayings 111 and 3b) or finding the imperial rule (sayings 20 and 49).

SAYING 57

The Father's imperial rule is like a person who had [good] seed. An enemy came by night and cast a weed among the good seed. They were not allowed to pluck the weed; they were told, "Lest you go to pluck the weed and pluck the wheat along with it. For at harvest the weeds will appear; they can be plucked and burned."

COMMENT

A much longer version of this story appears in Matt 13:24–30, where it is given an allegorical interpretation at 13:36–43, one of only three such fully developed allegorical interpretations of Jesus's stories in the canonical gospels. For the other two, see Matt 13:49–50; Matt 13:18–23 = Mark 4:13–20 = Luke 8:11–15. *Thomas*, as usual, offers no appended interpretations (see saying 1). For "imperial rule," see saying 20, and for the stories of Jesus (i.e., parables) in *Thomas*, see saying 9. For "the Father's imperial rule," see sayings 76a, 96, 97, and 98.

A gap exists in *Thomas*'s narrative that readers must fill in to make sense of the story. Between the owner (the "person having [good] seed") and the "weed" being cast among the [good] seed, a reader must understand that the enemy put a weed seed among the owner's good seed, and then both the good seed and the weed seed were sown in the field (cf. Matt 13:24). The fieldworkers, specified in Matthew (13:27), in *Thomas* are only indicated as an anonymous "they." In Matthew the enemy sows "weeds" (plural), but in *Thomas* only a (single) "weed" is sown, and it grows among the wheat, although "weeds" (plural) appear at the harvest.

Is the last statement in the story made by the narrator to the reader of *Thomas*, or is it stated to the fieldhands by the owner of the field? In Matthew the statement is clearly made to the workers (Matt 13:29–30). In Matthew's reading of the longer story, it references the end of the age when the righteous and the wicked are sorted out (13:36–43). Although *Thomas* mentions or alludes to "harvest" several times (sayings 21d, 45a, 63, and 73), the idea of an end of the age, such as is found in Paul (1 Cor 7:29–31), is not developed in *Thomas*. Some sayings may seem to suggest such a concept, however (sayings 10, 11a, 51, and 111); others, on the other hand, speak categorically against it (sayings 18 and 113). The focus of the story in *Thomas*'s version appears to be on the relative ease of recognizing weeds from wheat when they are fully developed, and the difficulty of recognizing the difference between them in seed form or in early germination. One might abstract this story's focus as: true character will eventually come out. (The Q saying that seems to express the same sentiment is Matt 7:16–17 = Luke 6:43–44.) This generalization, however, is not the exclusive "point" of the story since stories may have many "points" (see Hedrick, *Many Things in Parables*, 36–54).

Unlocking the Secrets of the *Gospel according to Thomas*

SAYING 58

Those who have suffered are favored; they have found life.

COMMENT

"To suffer": i.e., to experience pain, distress, difficulty, trouble, deep weariness, etc. Other translations are "labored," "struggled," "worked hard," and "toiled." On "favored," see saying 19a. No parallel to this macarism exists among the sayings attributed to Jesus (Matt 5:3–12; Luke 6:20b–23; Luke 11:28; John 20:29), although Matt 5:11–12 and Luke 6:22–23 reflect a situation of persecution. In *Thomas* the character of suffering is not specified. Other macarisms in *Thomas* are sayings 7, 19a, 49, 54, 68, 69a, 69b, 79a, 79b, and 103.

For the use of the unqualified word "life" in Thomas, see 4a. In early Christianity (Matt 7:14; 18:8–9; 19:17; Mark 9:43, 45; John 1:4; 3:36; 5:24, 26, 40; 6:33, 35, 48, 53, 63; 8:12; 10:10; 11:25; 14:6; 20:31; Rom 5:18; 8:2, 6; Phil 2:16; Col 3:4; 1 Tim 1:16; Jas 1:12), "life" is the equivalent of eternal life and the imperial rule (Mark 9:43, 47). Why suffering prompts the discovery of life in *Thomas* is unclear, but those who are marginalized from the mainstream of society have always been viewed with compassion in the Christian tradition (Matt 11:28–30 [and *Gos. Thom.* 90]; Luke 4:16–20; and cf. 1 Pet 2:19; Jas 1:27).

SAYING 59

While you are alive, look at the One-Who-Lives, lest you die and seek to see him and are not able to see.

COMMENT

The saying is a warning: the possibility of "seeing" the One-Who-Lives exists only during one's lifetime. For "the One-Who-Lives" (the living Father), see saying 37 (cf. prologue, and sayings 11a, 111). Early Christian tradition is divided on the issue of "seeing God": God cannot be seen: Exod 33:20–23; 1 Tim 6:15–16; John 1:18; 6:46; 1 John 4:20; Col 1:15; Heb 11:27. God can be seen: Job 42:5–6; Isa 6:1, 5; 38:11; Matt 5:8; Heb 12:14; Rev 20:11. "Seeing God": perhaps in an ecstatic theophany; cf. *Corp. herm.* 5; Dion. Ar. *d. n.* 1.597B; Dion. Ar. *c. h.* 4.180C; Dion. Ar. *ep.* 1.1065A/B; 5.1073A. Some argue that the One-Who-Lives is Jesus himself; but see the discussion in the prologue.

SAYING 60

<He saw> a Samaritan carrying a lamb as he was entering Judea. He said to his disciples, ("Why does) that fellow (carry) around the lamb?"
    They replied, "In order to kill and eat it."
    He replied, "While it is alive, he will not eat it, but (only) if he kills it and it becomes a carcass."
    They said, "He would not do otherwise."
    He said, "You should seek a place for yourselves in repose, lest you become a corpse and be eaten."

COMMENT

The text of this dialogue between Jesus and his disciples is partly corrupt. A main verb is lacking at the beginning of the dialogue, and the Coptic text of the question that Jesus initially asks his disciples is corrupt as well. The question, as reconstructed in the translation, seems required by the subsequent response of the disciples. Jesus initially asks the disciples what appears to be an innocuous question, but the answer to the question is far from obvious. There could be many reasons why a Samaritan enters Judea carrying a lamb. But the disciples, true to their character in *Thomas* (saying 22), state one obvious possibility: he intends to kill and eat it. Jesus's trite response seems to affirm their rationale: people don't eat live lambs; so he will make it a carcass and then eat it. And again the disciples, true to their character, agree with the obvious.

In the pronouncement at the end of the dialogue, however, Jesus elevates the conversation from the mundane, trite, and commonplace to a sophisticated spiritual level. The literal terms of the previous exchange (*alive, kill, eat, carcass*) in the pronouncement are charged with spiritual significance. A state of repose can be found now (sayings 50 and 51), but it is only found in the living Father (sayings 50 and 90), and life is only possible in the living Father (saying 11a). Apart from the living Father one is subjected to the negative influence of the "world" (saying 21c), which, as a "corpse" and "carcass" (sayings 56 and 80) "deadens" the spiritual senses (saying 28). The "world" will eventually "kill" the disciple and consume the corpse, for the "world" is an "eater of corpses" (*Gos. Phil.* 73:19–23). Even disciples can lose the little they have (*Gos. Thom.* 41).

SAYING 61A

Two will rest on a bed; one will die and the other live.

COMMENT

This saying has a Q parallel (Luke 17:34–35 = Matt 24:40–41). The literary context in which Luke includes it is a section on the end of the age (Luke 17:22–37). In such a context, the saying relates to the unexpected coming of the Son of Man (17:22, 30–31). Absent a literary context in *Thomas*, however, the saying simply affirms the uncertainty and capriciousness of human life. There is no obvious connection of the statement to saying 61b, but it shares some of the vocabulary of saying 60 ("rest," "die," "live"). A number of sayings in *Thomas* play on the numbers one and two (sayings 11b, 22, 23, 30, and 106).

SAYING 61B

Salome asked, "Who are you, fellow? Like somebody (important) you climbed upon my bed and ate from my table."
    Jesus replied, "I am from the Equality. I was endowed with what belongs to my Father."
    "I am your disciple."
    "Therefore I tell you: whoever becomes <equal> will be filled with light, but if divided, full of darkness."

COMMENT

For "Salome," cf. Mark 15:40; 16:1. For "Who are you?" cf. *Gos. Thom.* 43, 91 and 37. For "Like somebody important," the text may be corrupt, and translations differ.

    "Equality" in Jesus's first response literally means equal, level, or straight. The emendation in his second response is an obvious correction of a copyist's error. Equality for Plato was one of the eternal changeless forms, an absolute equality, known by the soul before birth. But in this world of change, there are only imperfect copies (Plato *Phaed.* 74–76). Aristotle (*Metaph.* x.3.3) argues that "equality" means unity—in other words, undividedness. The concept is picked up in ancient religious texts: The root of darkness is unequal or crooked (*Paraph. Shem* 2:14); its light is not equal to that of the Majesty (*Paraph. Shem* 9:17–19); Derdekeas "appeared for the sake of the clouds, because they are unequal, to end the wickedness of nature" (*Paraph. Shem* 39:24–29). A fiery light shines upon Hades in order that the equality of the faultless light might become apparent (*Paraph. Shem* 3:22–26; 10:16–17). "Being equal" is linked with imperishableness (*Eugnostos*: NHC III,3:78:9–12, and the parallels noted in Parrott, *Nag Hammadi*, 94–95). In other words, in *Thomas* the concept of "Equality" is linked with the living Father, the One-Who-Lives (saying 37), the self-originated light (saying 50), and in *Tri. Trac.* (132:16–28) it is blended with traditional Christian concepts. In *Thomas* Jesus is from the absolute Equality and has been endowed with the things of his Father (cf. John 3:35; 12:49; 15:15).

SAYING 62A

I tell my secrets to those who [seek my] secrets.

COMMENT

The text restored in this saying is usually restored as " . . . those who [are worthy of my] secrets." The present restoration is prompted by the primary strategy of *Thomas* in saying 1: that is, to encourage the experience of immortality by finding the interpretation of Jesus's words. See the sayings relating to seeking: 1, 2, 92, 94, and 110. Compare sayings relating to being worthy: 55, 56, 85, 111, 114; and sayings relating to revealing: 5, 6b, and 17.

In the New Testament, see Mark 4:11 = Matt 13:11 = Luke 8:10, where Jesus "communicates" "the secret" (or "secrets") of the imperial rule of God through parables. It is at best an oblique communication. In the early Christian communities the mystery (i.e., a "divine secret") was now an open secret (Rom 16:25–27; 1 Cor 2:7; 15:51; Eph 1:9–10; 3:3–10; 6:19; Col 1:24–28; 2:2; 4:3). Nevertheless, it still remains a mystery why God elected to pursue his purposes in that way. And some "mysteries" are not clear at all (Rom 11:25; Eph 5:28–32; 1 Tim 3:16).

SAYING 62B

Whatever your right hand does, don't let your left hand know.

COMMENT

The parallel saying in Matthew (6:3) is applied to giving alms (i.e., providing a charity gift), but in *Thomas* the saying appears without context. In Matthew the saying directs liberality in giving: i.e., don't keep account of your gifts of charity. But the saying in *Thomas* is an aphorism (see 4a), a terse statement of a principle or precept whose meaning is unclear on its surface. The subject of the saying is unclear, but it seems to be urging liberality in one's actions or single-mindedness in any endeavor. The reason that you don't let the left hand know what the right hand does is so that restrictions cannot be placed on what the right is doing, which is what Matt 6:3 advocates in the context of charitable giving. So the saying might be construed as follows: be absolutely committed. In the early Jesus movements the concept of absolute commitment was valued: Luke 9:62; 12:33; 14:33; Mark 10:21 = Matthew 19:21 = Luke 18:22; Mark 10:28 = Matt 19:27. Cf. *Gos. Thom.* 2, 55, and 76a.

SAYING 63

A rich person with great wealth said, "I will use my wealth to sow and reap, and plant, and fill my storehouses with produce, so that I lack nothing." The fellow intended to do this, yet during the night he died. Better pay attention to this.

COMMENT

A parallel to this story is found in Luke 12:16–20, and another in Sir 11:18–19. The stories in Luke and *Thomas* are not the same. Luke's protagonist is already a farmer, whose fields are overflowing at harvest time; *Thomas*'s protagonist is a wealthy investor who intends on becoming a farmer. Luke's story is unrealistic: the voice of God, unheard by the farmer, intrudes into the story addressing Luke's readers about the dangers of covetousness. The intrusion (Luke 12:20) is part of Luke's understanding of the story. The brief scenario depicted in *Thomas*'s story illustrates the uncertainty of mortal life and its impoverishment (compare sayings 28, 29, 56, 76b, and 110).

For a comparative analysis of all three stories, see the discussion in Hedrick, *Parables as Poetic Fictions*, 142–63; and *Many Things in Parables*, 95–99. For parables in *Thomas*, see saying 9. For "Better pay attention to this," see saying 8. For the negative view of "the world," see saying 21c.

SAYING 64A

A person was receiving visitors. When dinner was arranged, a slave was sent to invite the visitors. Going to the first, the slave said, "My master invites you."

He replied, "I have money for some merchants who will come to me in the evening. I will go and give my orders to them. I must decline the invitation to dinner."

He went to another and said, "My master invites you."

He replied, "I have purchased a house and am required for a day. I will have no time."

He went to another and said, "My master invites you."

He replied, "My friend is getting married, and I must arrange the dinner. I will be unable to come. I must ask to be excused from the dinner."

He went to another saying, "My master invites you."

He replied, "I have purchased some real estate and am going to collect the rents. I will not be able to come. I ask to be excused."

The slave came back and told his master, "Those you invited to dinner have excused themselves.

"The master told the slave, "Go out into the streets and whoever you find bring them to dine."

Better pay attention to this.

COMMENT

On parables in *Thomas*, see saying 9. This story appears in three versions: Matt 22:1–13//Luke 14:16–24//*Gos. Thom.* 64a. In each story the excuses offered are generally similar, but more similarity exists between *Thomas* and Luke in form and specifics of language. In *Thomas* the excuses offered by the visitors, excuses that ignore hospitality codes, relate to the conducting of business (ordering from merchants, purchasing property, collecting rents). In the third excuse (arranging a dinner for the marriage of a friend), the meal should likely be conceived as a catered affair, at least in part, and therefore is also generally related to "business." In the Hebrew Bible, under certain conditions absence from required social obligations is permitted (Deut 20:5–8; 24:5), but not in this case and for these reasons. Saying 64b, likely intended as a scribal interpretation of this narrative, strongly condemns business folk (i.e., the "buyers" and "sellers") in the narrative (cf. Sir 26:29—27:2). In terms of a general principle, the story affirms that the guests are too much involved with the "world" (sayings 21c and 56; Herm. *Sim.* 4.4.5-7; 8.8.1) and not with community obligations (i.e., the Thomasine community). In short, there are higher commitments in life, requiring single-minded devotion (see saying 16b). The children of the Light (saying 50) can be corrupted by the "world" and its concerns (Matt 18:7; Mark 4:18-19; Rom 12:2; 1 Cor 7:31-35; Gal 1:4; 2 Tim 4:10; Eph 2:2; Jas 1:27; 4:4; 2 Pet 1:4; 2:20; 1 John 2:15-16; 5:19).

For "Better pay attention to this," see saying 8.

SAYING 64B

Buyers and [sellers will] not [enter] my Father's places.

COMMENT

See the discussion in saying 64a.

SAYING 65

A [. . .] person had a vineyard. He let it out to some farmers to work so he could receive from them his produce. He sent his slave to collect the vineyard's produce from the farmers. They grabbed the slave, beat him, and nearly killed him. The slave returned and reported to his master. His master said, "Perhaps he did not know them."

He sent another slave. The farmers beat this other one. Then the master sent his son, saying, "Perhaps they will respect my son."

Since those farmers knew he was the heir of the vineyard, they grabbed him and killed him.

Better pay attention to this.

COMMENT

The word left in lacuna has been restored in two ways, both of which are possible. The usual restoration is ⲚⲬⲢⲎ[ⲤⲦⲞ]Ⲥ, having a meaning of "good" (hence a "good person"), but the text in the lacuna may also be restored ⲚⲬⲢⲎ[ⲤⲦⲎ]Ⲥ, meaning a "creditor" or "usurer" (i.e., a moneylender; Kloppenborg, *Tenants in the Vineyard*, 249). So the story either begins "a good person," or "a moneylender." Either restoration will slant the reading of the narrative in a particular direction.

"Receive from them 'his' produce": that is, the property owner's share of the produce, rather than all the produce of the vineyard. But it could be translated "its" fruit and in that case the slave demands all the produce of the vineyard (see Plisch, *Gospel of Thomas*, 162). "Perhaps he did not know them": The number of the pronouns should likely be reversed to read "perhaps *they* did not know *him*" (i.e., so that the reference is to the farmers who fail to recognize the slave), unless the master is thinking that the slave did not know the farmers. The following makes better sense, however: "Perhaps they [i.e., the farmers] did not know him [i.e., the slave]," since up to this point in the narrative multiple farmers have mistreated a single slave. What the reader should make of the fact that the tenants are "farmers" rather than vintners (ἀμπελουργός, or its equivalent in Coptic) is unclear. The story has a parallel in the New Testament: Mark 12:1–9 = Matt 21:33–41 = Luke 20:9–16.

Translation and Commentary

Numerous differences exist between the canonical tradition and *Thomas*. For example, Mark's version portrays numerous slaves being sent, some of whom were beaten and others killed. Matthew and Luke reduce the number of times slaves are sent, and neither describes any of them being killed. In *Thomas*, only two slaves are sent, and neither one is killed. The canonical versions are cast as allegories (for discussion of allegory, see sayings 9, 20, and 21a), but those specific allegorical features are lacking in *Thomas* (see Jeremias, *Parables of Jesus*, 70–77).

The story as a whole reflects some of the risks faced by absentee landowners in Palestine (see Kloppenborg, *Tenants in the Vineyard*, 38–40, 279–81). The farmers kill the owner's son because they know that he is the owner's heir, and they hope that the property will be abandoned. But that would hardly be *Thomas*'s interest in the narrative. Likely, *Thomas* was interested in the story because it illustrates the hazards of involvement with the "world" (see the discussion in saying 64a).

For "Better pay attention to this," see saying 8.

SAYING 66

Teach me about the stone the builders rejected—it is the cornerstone.

COMMENT

Saying 66 is introduced by "Jesus said" in *Thomas*, making it an independent saying from saying 65, which already has a concluding statement ("Better pay attention to this"). But saying 66, originally known from Ps 118:22, is used in early Christian texts (Acts 4:11; 1 Pet 2:7; *Barn.* 6.4) as a christological allusion, and is so used on the lips of Jesus at the conclusion of the parable of the vineyard (Mark 12:10 = Matt 21:42 = Luke 20:17). Its association here with the version of the story in *Thomas* prompts many interpreters to argue that the two sayings were originally related. But that does not appear to be the case, to judge from the way *Thomas* treats it (i.e., including it as a separate saying with its own introduction). The saying is enigmatic. For example, in Mark, the parable and the saying enrage the Jewish authorities, and they try to arrest Jesus because "they perceived the parable" (and hence the saying) "was told against them" (12:12). In Matthew the parable and the saying are related to Judaism's loss of the kingdom of God (21:43, 45). Luke concludes with a specific interpretation of the saying that is as enigmatic as the saying itself (20:18; but cf. *Barn.* 6.2). So the three evangelists do not draw overt christological applications from the saying. The Naasenes interpreted the "stone" as Adam (Hippolytus *Ref.* 5.7.35).

The saying appears to have a proverbial character: those who are supposed to know how to construct buildings don't even recognize the value and function of the one stone that holds the entire edifice together. So the question becomes: What does the collector in *Thomas* regard as the rejected stone that holds everything together? Likely it is the gospel proclaimed by the living Jesus (see sayings 3a, 3b, 16a, 16b, and 28). It is rather odd to have Jesus requesting to be taught, but compare the following sayings where Jesus asks questions for information (sayings 13, 60, 72, and 78).

SAYING 67

Whoever knows everything, and is wanting in one thing, is lacking in every way.

COMMENT

The saying contrasts knowledge of everything (i.e., the whole, the universe) with completeness or fullness (i.e., nothing lacking). In other words one is completely "full" or is totally "deficient." Plisch thinks the saying does not presume the missing element to be anything specific (*Gospel of Thomas*, 164). Meyer (*Gospel of Thomas*, 95), on the other hand, thinks that the deficiency is a spiritual deficiency (i.e., a deficiency of light, of the spirit of God, etc.). Sayings attributed to Jesus make a similar point about "fullness": Matt 5:48; Matt 19:21 (cf. Mark 10:21 = Luke 18:22). Fullness or completeness is also a concern of the early followers of Jesus (1 Cor 13:2; Phil 3:15; Eph 4:13; Col 4:12). And there is the suggestion that failing to be fully complete is a "spiritual deficiency" because of the standard they held before themselves (John 1:16; Eph 1:23; 3:19; 4:13; Col 1:19; 2:9). See the discussion of deficiency and poverty in *Thomas* (sayings 54, 41, 70, and 63). Likely the compiler of the text would understand what is lacking to be a particular spiritual dimension (see sayings 3b and 29) even though the language of the saying does not specifically demand such an understanding. In any case, the *Thomas* saying holds forth an extreme standard: even one thing lacking will invalidate the whole.

SAYING 68

You are favored when hated and persecuted, and (when) no place will be found where you have been persecuted.

COMMENT

On "favored," see saying 19a. This macarism consists of three segments, two of which are negative (hated and persecuted) and a contrasting third that is positive (not persecuted anywhere). Some think that the saying may be corrupt and suspect that the third segment should be negative (and no place will be found where you are not persecuted). A negative appears in a similar statement in Clement (*Strom.* 4.6.41 it reads: ". . . they will have a place where they will not be persecuted"). In *Thomas*, on the other hand, the saying affirms the complete absence of persecution. Making the third segment negative, in effect, turns an antithetical parallel into a synonymous parallel. Both are forms of Hebrew poetry.

Parallels to the idea that you are favored when hated and persecuted are found in Matt 5:10 and Q (Matt 5:11 = Luke 6:22), *Thomas* (sayings 58 and 69a) and elsewhere (see DeConick, *Original Gospel of Thomas*, 220–22). *Thomas* in an antithetical parallelism, however, promises that the auditors remain favored in times of both persecution and toleration. Luke 6:26 warns against general acceptance. For other parallelisms in *Thomas*, see 4b, 11a, 27. *Thomas* affirms that the followers of Jesus are favored both when they are persecuted and when they are not.

SAYING 69A

Those who have been persecuted in their heart are favored; they have truly known the Father.

COMMENT

"Favored," see saying 19a. A parallel in Clement of Alexandria (*Quis div.* 25) makes a contrast between exterior persecution by others (as in *Gos. Thom.* 68, above) and a kind of interior persecution in which one is pursued by "impious lusts, diverse pleasures, base hopes and destructive dreams" (see DeConick, *Original Gospel of Thomas*, 223). The idea that the human heart is conflicted is widely recognized in early Christian tradition (Mark 7:20–22 = Matt 15:18–19; Matt 5:28; Luke 1:51; 6:45; Heb 3:12; Jas 4:8; *Teach. Silv.* 84:15—85:21). In the final analysis, only the person who overcomes these "persecutions" will see God (Matt 5:8; see the discussion of *Gos. Thom.* 27).

On "knowing the Father," see saying 3b.

SAYING 69B

Those who go hungry to fill the starving belly of another are favored.

COMMENT

"Favored," see saying 19a. This macarism expresses sentiments unusual for *Thomas*, since it focuses on meeting an actual physical need. The status of "favored one" is for the individual who hungers in order to satisfy the hunger of another. In short, the saying is more like Luke 6:21 than Matt 5:6. Such altruistic behavior, rather than ritual behavior (see sayings 6a, 14a, 53), defines for *Thomas* what the essence of true religion is. The same concern for the needs of others is a strong part of early Christian tradition (Matt 25:35–40; Jas 1:27; and see further parallels in *Thomas* 36). "The starving belly of another," literally means, "the belly of one who desires."

SAYING 70

What you generate within yourselves will save you;
  the lack of it [will] kill you.

COMMENT

Coming to know oneself is the essence of "salvation" in *Thomas* (saying 3b). It is how one comes to know one's divine origins and how one comes to be known by God (see saying 111). Without this self-knowledge, which brings about knowledge of one's divine origins, one exists in poverty and is poverty (sayings 29, 3b).

SAYING 71

I will [. . .] and no one will be able [. . .].

COMMENT

The first lacuna of this saying is usually restored: "I will [destroy this] house and no one will be able to build it [. . . .]." The second lacuna has been restored as "to build it [again]" or "to rebuild it [except me]." I have left the lacunae blank since the restorations are highly questionable. For some, "this house" in the restored first part of the saying is the Jerusalem temple, and parallels are found in Matt 26:61; 27:40; Mark 14:58; and John 2:19. Yet none of these parallels portray Jesus saying that he will destroy the temple—only that some heard him say such a thing. The parallel in John does quote Jesus, but in the Johannine saying Jesus does not threaten to destroy the temple, rather he promises to rebuild the temple if it is destroyed. No parallels have been cited for the second half of the saying that would provide a clue to its restoration, and there is no general agreement for the meaning of the restored saying (see Plisch, *Gospel of Thomas*, 70–72).

If the restoration of the first half of the saying is accurate, then the saying in *Thomas* is the only instance of the saying on Jesus's lips. Assuming the restoration is correct, what could it possibly mean? Perhaps a clue can be found from the uses of *house* in *Thomas*: a family unit (sayings 16b and 48); a building that houses the family (sayings 21b, 35 [bis], and 64a); a home (sayings 97 and 98); the residence of a titular head of a family unit (saying 35). "House" in *Thomas* appears to be related to the nuclear family unit, which the living Jesus aims to put in disarray (saying 16b) and turn upside down (saying 22).

SAYING 72

[Someone said] to him, "Tell my brothers to divide my father's things with me."

He replied, "Fellow, who made me a divider?" He turned to his disciples and said, "I am not a divider, am I?"

COMMENT

This same scene is found in Luke 12:13-14, where it serves to introduce the story about the rich fool (Luke 12:15-21). In *Thomas*, however, it is an independent *chreia*, a short literary form in which a pointed saying of general significance attributed to a definite person arises out of a particular situation. The response in Luke ("Fellow, who made me a judge or divider over you?"), which is also found in *Thomas*, is closely tied to the situation; but in *Thomas* the final statement, lacking in Luke, has general significance ("I am not a divider, am I?"). This saying is not found attributed to Jesus elsewhere in early Christian literature. *Thomas* also features the story of the rich farmer (saying 63), separately from the *chreia*. Luke's story (cf. *Gos. Thom.* 63) appears to be a Lukan adaptation of an earlier version of the story of the rich farmer (see Hedrick, *Parables as Poetic Fictions*, 142-44; *Many Things in Parables*, 95-99), although not everyone agrees.

The issue raised in saying 72 and in Luke has roots in Jewish tradition, where "dividers," or judges, served as objective executors for property settlements (Exod 2:14; Prov 17:2; Luke 18:2-5; Acts 7:27-28, 35; m. Bek. 4:6). Saying 72 is something of a conundrum. The way the question is put demands a simple yes-or-no answer, but the evidence from *Thomas* about Jesus's being a "divider" is mixed. In *Thomas* Jesus is portrayed as both divider and "unifier." As divider, he comes to throw divisions upon the earth (saying 16a), dividing families (sayings 55 and 101), and polarizing allegiances (sayings 100 and 47a). On the other hand, as unifier he eradicates divisions (saying 23); he unifies "houses" (saying 48); he brings "light," as the promise of equality and unity (saying 61b); he empowers through unity (saying 106); and he unifies the divided human sexual condition by making it whole again (saying 114). Hence the question is a riddle (see Judg 14:10-18). For the spiritually enlightened, it cannot be answered with a simple yes or no, for they see both sides of Jesus's activity. The unenlightened, however, see only the obvious side—his divisive activity—and therefore answer the question easily—but wrongly! The spiritual person possessing the key remains silent, as do the wise (see Sir 20:1–7; Eccl 3:7).

SAYING 73

The harvest is great but workers are few. So then beg the master to send forth workers into the harvest.

COMMENT

The Q saying paralleling *Thomas* 73 is virtually identical in Matthew (9:37–38) and Luke (10:2), and very close to *Thomas* as well. The differences are that Q reads "lord of the harvest" (for *foreman, owner*), and *Thomas* reads only "master" (*owner*). Q reads "therefore" (οὖν), and *Thomas* reads "so then" (δέ). The harvest image also appears in the following sayings in *Thomas*: 9, 21d, 57, and 63. It is a serviceable image in antiquity, appearing in sayings involving divine judgment (Jer 12:13; Hos 10:10–15; Job 4:8–9), joy and sadness (Ps 126:5–6), evangelism (John 4:35–38; *Gos. Phil.* 55:19–22), stewardship (2 Cor 9:6–12), faithful service (Gal 6:7–9), apocalyptic (Rev 14:14–20), and allegory (*Gos. Phil.* 52:25–35; Matt 13:37–43). In this case, the appeal for more workers seems more likely to refer to evangelism (see saying 33a for other *Thomas* sayings related to evangelism).

Sayings 73–76a share a contrast between the many and the few (see saying 8), and some commentators have suggested that sayings 73–75 form a short dialogue.

SAYING 74

Someone said, "Lord, many are around the well, but nothing is in the well."

COMMENT

"Nothing" can also be translated "no one." In *Thomas*, this saying is addressed to the "Lord" (i.e., Jesus) by an anonymous figure. It appears to be a casual remark about an empty well (or cistern) to which people have come seeking water. The difference between a well and cistern is often not apparent (Prov 5:15; Isa 30:14; Jer 14:3); hence the Coptic word in this saying refers to either well or cistern. A cistern is a receptacle hewed out of rock or a pit dug in the earth whose bottom and sides have been plastered. A well is a pit dug in the earth to provide access to underground water. Both receptacles are used to catch and store rain water. In a desert climate, potable water means the difference between living and dying, and hence enables life in desert places. Thus, the water is used figuratively to represent an essential resource of life (Prov 10:11; John 4:14). The well and cistern are also used negatively to represent the failed foreign gods Israel trusted rather than trusting in Yahweh (Jer 2:13; 14:3–4). But Jesus's interlocutor sees nothing more than an empty well. The saying also appears in Origen (*Cels.* 8.15–16), where Celsus is thought by Origin to be citing some unknown heretical sect from a book they produced, titled *A Heavenly Dialogue*. Saying 75 (below) appears to be the second half of the dialogue in which Jesus responds to the statement about the well.

For the *many/few* contrast in sayings 73–76a, see saying 8. See the discussion in Plisch (*Gospel of Thomas*, 176–78) for the problems in saying 74. For the motif of emptiness and poverty, see saying 29.

SAYING 75

Jesus replied, "Many stand at the door, but the solitary ones will enter the wedding chamber."

COMMENT

Saying 75 is most likely the response to the anonymous interlocutor of saying 74. In *Thomas* the responses of Jesus sometimes appear to be oblique; i.e., not a direct answer to the question or statement (see sayings 24, 79a, and 104). See saying 22 in reference to the different levels of understanding between Jesus and his interlocutors.

In saying 74 (above), the interlocutor is concerned about the crowd around the well (whether of animals or people is unclear) and the absence of anything in the well. In this saying, Jesus raises the level of the discussion to a spiritual plane about the few who will enter the "wedding chamber," that is, about those who will "find the imperial reign" (saying 49), or achieve the ultimate state of salvation (for more about the meaning of "solitary," see saying 16b). In the Manichaean interpretation of the story of the ten maidens (Matt 25:1–12), the bride is the soul and the bridegroom is Jesus, or alternatively the bride is the church and the bridegroom is the mind (Allberry, *Manichaean Psalm-Book*, 154, 1–12). Apparently the purified soul (feminine in Greek) is united with Jesus in the bridal chamber (Allberry, *Manichaean Psalm-Book*, 263:17–19, 29; 264:13). See Gos. Thom. 104; *Exeg. Soul* 132:6—133:6; *Auth. Teach.* 34:1–18; Gos. Phil. 69:1—70:4 and 81:34—85:26. In Valentinianism the return to the androgynous state of creation occurs in the bridal chamber (*Gos. Phil.* 70:9–22; Gen 2:24; Mark 10:6–8; Gos. Thom. 22; 104). In *Thomas* only the elect actually achieve that state.

For the *many/few* contrast in 73–76a, see saying 8.

Unlocking the Secrets of the *Gospel according to Thomas*

SAYING 76A

The Father's imperial rule is like a merchant with merchandise who found a pearl. That merchant was wise; he sold the merchandise and bought the single pearl for himself.

COMMENT

This parable has a parallel in Matt 13:45–46. The major differences between the versions include the following: *Thomas*'s merchant is described as "wise" (other translations read "shrewd," "prudent," or "thoughtful"); Matthew's pearl is described as having great value; Matthew's narrative emphasizes that the merchant sold all his merchandise in order to purchase the pearl; Matthew's merchant is described as engaged in seeking "fine pearls," whereas *Thomas*'s merchant appears to have simply stumbled across a single pearl. Commercial ventures (sayings 64a, 64b, and 65) are described negatively in *Thomas*, and merchants in particular are described rather harshly (saying 64a). We must assume, therefore, that the positive characterization of this merchant is due to the spiritual insight that leads to the acquisition of the "single" or "solitary" pearl (see saying 16b for the high importance of singularity and *solitary* in *Thomas*; and sayings 55 and 62b, which stress single-mindedness in the pursuit of a goal). For the *many/few* contrast in sayings 73–76a, see saying 8.

Saying 76b, although elsewhere cast as a discrete saying, is here cast as the interpretation to the pearl parable (see saying 9 for a discussion of parables). Compare the similarity of the Matthean version of the hidden-treasure parable (13:44) to Matthew's parable of the pearl (*Gos. Thom.* 109).

SAYING 76B

Seek the imperishable and enduring treasure,
  where no moth threatens to devour,
  and no worm destroys.

COMMENT

The Q parallel to this saying (Luke 12:33 = Matt 6:20) is rather different: Matthew has, "lay up ... treasures in heaven where neither moth nor rust ... and thieves ..."; Luke has, "... provide ... unfailing treasure in the heavens where ... no thief ... no moth ..."

This saying encourages the abandonment of worldly affairs (cf. sayings 76a, 56, 63, and 110) and the single-minded pursuit of the eternal treasure, which is the imperial rule (saying 49). These motifs are basic to the early Christian faiths (for example, Matt 6:33 = Luke 12:31; Luke 9:62).

For the tradition history of this saying see Johnson, *Imperishable Treasure*.

Unlocking the Secrets of the *Gospel according to Thomas*

SAYING 77A

I am the Light over all.
  I am the all.
Everything came forth from me.
  Everything attained to me.

COMMENT

For "the light over all," see *Gos. Thom.* 50 and John 8:12; 9:5; 12:46. In lines 1 and 2 of the poetic arrangement of this saying, "the all" is the sum total of everything: the universe, the entirety of all things. Lines 3 and 4 are another way of affirming "I am the beginning and the end of all things," i.e., their origin and their point of return (Rom 11:36; Rev 21:6; 22:13; 1 Cor 8:6; and *Gos. Thom.* 18). The highest christological statement in early Christian literature, Col 1:15–20, captures the essence of this saying (cf. Col 3:11; 1 Cor 15:28). In other words, all things originated with the Light and found their convergence in the Light. The vista provided by this saying is so great that Jesus is encroaching on the role of the Father (cf. prologue and sayings 37, 50, and 59; John 1:1–4), as already is the case in Col 1:15–20. In *Acts Pet.* 39 (end of second century) Peter says to Jesus, "You are the all and the all is in you . . ."

For use of the image of light, see sayings 24, 61b, and 83. And for occurrences of "the all" (i.e., "everything"), see saying 67.

SAYING 77B

Split a piece of wood; I am there. Take up a stone and you will find me there.

COMMENT

This saying also appears in fragmentary form in the Greek version of saying 30 (see Layton, *Nag Hammadi*, 119–20, 127), where the two strands of the saying appear in reverse order. Hence the saying is treated here as a saying distinct from saying 77a. The *Thomas* saying reflects a panentheistic concept: i.e., the speaker permeates all things but still remains "I"—that is, distinct from all things. Compare the following similar sayings: Col 1:17; Heb 1:3; Eph 1:22–23; 4:6, 10.

SAYING 78

Why did you come into the countryside? To see a reed moved by the wind? To see someone wearing soft garments [like your] kings and nobles? They wear soft garments and [will] not be able to recognize the truth.

COMMENT

This saying has a Q parallel (Luke 7:24–25 = Matt 11:7–8), but the *Thomas* version is more compact. *Thomas* makes a comparison between the coarseness of life in the country and the high lifestyle of the king's court (represented by the "softness" of the garments of the wealthy), which is clearer in the expanded context of the Q saying (Luke 7:24–28 = Matt 11:7–11), where the Q saying refers to John the Baptist (see Mark 1:6). In *Thomas*, the saying takes on a more general character: people looking for "truth" don't find it in the politically expedient "king's court," where allegiances change like the wind with each new intrigue. The saying reflects a disdain for centers of political power and it encourages auditors to seek truth in the common places of life (see sayings 3a and 3b, 113). Kings and powerful nobles do not know "truth," for they have invested themselves in "the world" (sayings 21c, 64a, and 64b; John 18:38a). The saying reflects a general prejudice on the part of the poor (see saying 54) against the rich and powerful, or the attitude of an in-group (see saying 40) sensing itself marginalized from the centers of power (see sayings 69a, 81, and 110).

For great ones (Matt 20:25; Rev 6:15) such as nobles, see saying 98. The word "truth" as an absolute appears few times in *Thomas*: twice in the attributive position (sayings 53 and 101), in the absolute sense (saying 78), once as a scribe's error (saying 6a), and twice adverbially (saying 69a and 79a).

SAYING 79A

A woman in the crowd said to him, "The womb that bore you and the breasts that nourished you are favored."
    He replied, "Those who heeded the Father's word and truly kept it are favored."

COMMENT

This short chreia (see saying 72) has a close parallel in Luke 11:27–28. In the saying Jesus deflects an accolade intended for both him and his mother from a woman in the crowd. "Favored," see saying 19a. Because of his standing in the community, his mother is also favored for having borne such a son (cf. Luke 1:42, 48). But Jesus elevates the discourse to a spiritual level by insisting that only those obedient to God are blessed (for other such global shifts in the level of discourse between Jesus and his interlocutors see sayings 22, 74, and 75).

    For the general concept of obedience in *Thomas*, see saying 99. A similar macarism on those obedient to God is found in John 13:17 and Jas 1:25. The nature of the Father's word (written? oral?) is not specified.

Unlocking the Secrets of the *Gospel according to Thomas*

SAYING 79B

For days will come when you say, "The womb not having conceived and the breasts not having nursed are favored."

COMMENT

This saying is paralleled by Luke 23:29, which in the context of Luke 23:27–31 appears to be a prediction of some dire calamity. Similar sayings in Mark 13:17–19 = Matt 24:19–21 = Luke 21:23–24 are also part of a similar warning. "Favored," see saying 19a. In such a context, not bearing children and so not exposing them to suffering such indignities is the wise course of action (cf. 1 Macc 1:59–61). In the present arrangement in *Thomas* with saying 79b immediately following 79a, the point of 79b seems to be that there are other spiritual realities that are much more important than natural generation. In other words, obedience to "the word of the Father," which in this text would likely be pursuing with undivided devotion the imperial rule of the Father (sayings 2 and 99); such a pursuit becomes the prime directive over that of obedience to the command to be fruitful (Gen 1:28).

Some scholars have suggested a negative view of sexuality in the arrangement of sayings 79a and 79b (Meyer, *Gospel of Thomas*, 99; Grant and Schoedel, *Secret Sayings of Jesus*, 173–74). But see a similar way of handling the obligations of obedience to a religious vision and family obligations in Paul's advice to the Corinthian community (1 Cor 7:1–40).

SAYING 80

Whoever has known the world has discovered the body; the world is unworthy of such a person.

COMMENT

See the discussion of saying 56, which is a doublet of this saying.

SAYING 81

Let the wealthy rule, and the powerful decline (to rule).

COMMENT

The powerful should decline to rule the state. But the powerful are obsessed with power, so it is unlikely that they would decline the opportunity to rule—one maintains power by exercising it. And those normally described as the wealthy are focused on amassing wealth (compare saying 64a). It is a puzzling saying that mandates a shift in the focus of the two most influential classes in society, and also seems to contradict values that are rather clear in *Thomas*. For example, *Thomas* argues against involvement in the affairs of the world (sayings 21c, 64a, and 64b), and has already dismissed both the wealthy and the powerful for failing to recognize the truth (saying 78), presumably because of their involvement with the world (saying 64a). In other words, the "wealthy" who should become kings (i.e., reign) are not the materially wealthy (*Gos. Thom.* 110; Jas 5:1–6; 2 Cor 6:10; 8:9; Luke 12:21; Rev 2:9), but those with an inner spiritual wealth (Jas 2:5). They are the sons of the Living One, who have come to know themselves (saying 3b); they are the solitaries (saying 16b), who never stopped seeking till they found a great discovery (saying 2), which is the imperial rule within themselves (saying 49). The solitary's power (sayings 48, 106) and wealth, which is the knowledge of the self and the awareness of the divine within (saying 108), exceeds that of Adam (saying 85).

The idea of "reigning" and "becoming kings" is already present among the earliest followers of Jesus (1 Cor 4:8; 2 Tim 2:12). There is an apparent parallel to the second half of the saying in *Dial. Sav.* 129:13–14: "I tell you that '[....] power renounce [....].'"

SAYING 82

Whoever is near me is near the fire, and whoever is far from me is far from the imperial rule.

COMMENT

This saying has several parallels (see Hedrick, "Anecdotal Argument," 118–24; and Plisch, *Gospel of Thomas*, 189–91). Two of the earliest are: Origen *Hom. Jer.* 20.3 (second century) and *Gos. Sav.* 107:43–48 (second century). The saying draws an antithetical parallel between fire and the imperial rule. That is to say, a person close to Jesus is near to fire/the imperial rule, and conversely, a person at a distance from Jesus is far from the fire/the imperial rule. In *Thomas*, the imperial rule is the ultimate goal of the spiritual person (saying 49), and represents the presence of God.

In the Hebrew Bible fire is associated with God's judgment (Gen 19:24; Exod 9:23–24; Isa 33:10–14), as a means of purification (Lev 13:52; Num 31:23), or discernment (Jer 23:28–32). But it is also associated with God's presence and protection to the extent that God could be referred to with the epithet "fire" (Deut 4:24; Zech 2:5; Isa 10:16–17; cf. Heb 12:29) and described using language related to fire (for example: Deut 9:3; Ps 18:6–9). The Deuteronomist writes: "For Yahweh your God is a consuming fire" (Deut 4:24). Yahweh appeared to Moses as a flame of fire (Exod 3:2). He guided the Israelites out of Egypt in a pillar of fire (Exod 13:21–22) and appeared to them in fire (Exod 19:18). Thus, fire may be considered a characteristic theophanic manifestation of Yahweh in Hebrew Scripture.

As in saying 77a, in saying 82 Jesus makes a claim to a close relationship to the Father, similar to statements in the Gospel of John (for example, John 10:30; 14:9). See saying 37 and the prologue for the relationship of Father and Son in *Thomas*. See saying 10 for more about the image of fire.

SAYING 83

Images are apparent to people;
  yet the light in them is concealed in the image of the Father's light.
He will be revealed;
  yet his image remains concealed by his light.

COMMENT

The saying is composed of two parallel assertions, with the second building on the first. The first deals with "images" that are apparent to everyone, although their "light" is nevertheless concealed by the image of the Father's "light" (light is required for images to be visible [*Gos. Phil.* 69:8–14], and this light derives ultimately from the Father of Light in the intelligible world). In the second assertion the revelation of the Father works in a similar way: he will be revealed, although in this revelation too his "image" is concealed by his light, which is itself an image. The images "apparent to everyone" in the first assertion are likely images reproduced in a mirror, in a portrait, in water, or in shadows (see saying 84). In Platonic thought the images of the visible world are not the reality itself, but in the visible world one sees merely semblances of the reality in the intelligible world. Everything about us in the visible world is but a pale imitation of what exists perfectly in an intelligible world of ideas and forms (Plato *Resp.* 6.20 [509C–511A]; 7.1–2:5 [14A–517A]). The *Thomas* saying asserts that images cannot be seen apart from the Father's light (compare Plato's simile of the sun: Plato *Res.* 6.17–19 [507C–509B]): that is, the sun (which is a semblance of the light in the intelligible world) renders all things (i.e., the images in the visible world) visible to the natural eye just as Plato's Good (in the case of *Thomas*, the Good equals the Father) makes it possible to recognize the difference between the visible world of illusion and the intelligible world of ideas.

The second assertion affirms that the Father will be revealed, even though his "image" always remains concealed by his light. Or stated in biblical language, no one has ever seen God (Exod 24:16–17; 33:17–23; Ezek 1:26–28; John 1:18; 1 John 4:12; 1 Tim 1:17; 6:16; Heb 11:27; Rev 4:3–5; 21:23; 22:5). A similar distinction between visible (i.e., earthly) and intelligible (i.e., heavenly) worlds is shared by Philo (*Alleg. Interp.* 1.31–32) and the early followers of Jesus (Rom 1:21–23; 2 Cor 4:3–4; Col 1:15; Heb 10:1). The *Thomas* saying reassures readers that the Living Father will be adequately revealed even though the visible world remains a place of illusion.

On "revealing," see sayings 5, 6b, 17, 37, 62a, 108; on "light," see sayings 24, 61b, 50, 77a. On "image," see sayings 22, 50, and 84.

SAYING 84

When you see your likeness, you rejoice. But when you see your images that came into being before you, and they neither die nor appear, how much will you endure?

COMMENT

See saying 83. The first statement refers to the feeling of satisfaction people experience upon seeing their personal reflection (in mirror, water, or portrait). The second statement describes immortal and invisible "images" (Davies, *Gospel of Thomas*, 107), which are the forms and types of all things in the visible world (Plato *Tim.* 51B–52C; and *Gos. Thom.* 83). When people "see" these images (i.e., perceive their existence in the intelligible world—*see* is a metaphorical use of the Coptic word; compare *Gos. Thom.* 111; *Gos. Phil.* 54:19; John 20:8; Heb 11:5), they become disturbed (saying 2). This prompts the question: How much of this kind of information can one endure? Viewing our physical image brings delight, but perceiving our eternal image in the intelligible world brings distress because of our human imperfections in comparison to it. Sayings 83 and 84 are heavily influenced by a kind of thinking that derives ultimately from Platonic thought (see the discussion in Plisch, *Gospsel of Thomas*, 193–94).

SAYING 85

Adam came into being from a great power and a great wealth; yet he was not [worthy] of you. Had he been worthy [he would] not [have] died.

COMMENT

In the second account of creation (Gen 2:4b–7), Adam is the first of God's creative acts. In the first account (Gen 1:26–31), Adam is the final act of the creative process. Nevertheless, in spite of his exalted status as the first human being, and in spite of the fact that he was created in the image of God (Gen 1:26–27), he is not worthy of "you" (i.e., of those who have discovered the true meaning of the sayings of Jesus), for Adam died (Gen 3:17–19). Those addressed in this saying ("you"), on the other hand, having discovered the true meaning of Jesus's words, will never die (saying 1). There is a subtle contrast between Adam's origin in great power and wealth, and the children of the Light (sayings 50 and 37), who, having found themselves in a great poverty (saying 29), nevertheless have discovered the imperial rule (saying 49) and achieved immortality.

Adam and John the Baptizer (saying 46) were worthy figures of a previous order and for that reason are held in esteem by the Thomasine community; therefore, Jesus could refer to himself as a child of Adam (86) and to his followers as Adam's children (106). Paul regarded Adam negatively because of his sin (Rom 5:14; 1 Cor 15:22), but a Pauline disciple absolves Adam of responsibility for the sin that removed him from paradise (1 Tim 2:13–14). In *Apoc. Mos.* 39:1–3, God promises to raise Adam up to enjoy the benefits of paradise again, and restores him to paradise in the third heaven (37:4–6).

For "worthy," see sayings 55, 56, 80, 111, 114, and 62a. For "immortality," see saying 19c.

SAYING 86

[Foxes have their dens] and birds [their] nests, but Adam's child has no place to lay his head and rest.

COMMENT

This saying has a Q parallel, which is identical in Matthew and Luke (Luke 9:58 = Matt 8:20). The only difference between *Thomas* and the Q version is that *Thomas* adds "and rest" at the end. It is unclear whether this difference is a performancial variation (i.e., "resting" is a naturally included idea in "laying one's head down" and hence is merely a variation in performance), or if it is a hermeneutical variation (i.e., a variation that interprets the saying in a certain tendentious direction). In some *Thomas* sayings, the idea of "resting" is idealized as "heavenly rest" or salvation (sayings 50, 51, 60, 90; cf. 61a), rather than being simply a time of physical recuperation after a period of strenuous activity.

The language of saying 86 suggests a situation of itinerancy and exclusion from normal society. Both concepts figure prominently in *Thomas*: itinerancy (sayings 14b, 36, and 42 [on some readings]); exclusion (sayings 27, 78, and 81). The term "Adam's child" (usually, "son of man") is a self-referential term attributed to Jesus in the gospels (for example, Mark 2:27–28). In the Hebrew Scriptures, the term "son of man" is used in three ways: to describe the insignificance of human beings (Job 25:4–6), to describe the exalted status of human beings (Ps 8:3–6), and to describe a future apocalyptic figure (Dan 7:13–14; cf. Mark 8:38; 13:26; 14:62). In saying 86, the term seems equivalent to "an insignificant human being," judging by the contrast with wild animals. In *Thomas* the terms "child of Adam" and "children of Adam" in saying 106 are positive, apparently as equivalent to "children of light" (sayings 3b and 50, cf. 85).

SAYING 87

Wretched is the body dependent on a body, and wretched is the soul dependent on both of these.

COMMENT

No New Testament parallels exist for this saying, but a related saying is found in *Gos. Thom.* 112 (below). Saying 87 is in the form of a "woe," the opposite of a macarism (see Rev 3:17 for a description of a wretched state, and see Luke 6:24–26 for examples of woes). Commentators have found the saying difficult, and no agreement on a reasonable sense for the saying has emerged in the discussion. Considering the word "body" (Greek: σῶμα or Coptic: ⲥⲱⲙⲁ) as metonymy for the whole person (see Schweizer, "Σῶμα, σωματικός, σύσσωμος," *TDNT*, 7.1032, 7.1058–59; see also Mark 5:29, 14:22; Luke 12:4) makes possible a reasonable sense: "a person dependent on a person." A person dependent on another works against the philosophy of *Thomas*, which stresses solitariness (sayings 16b and 49) and making the two one (sayings 4b, 22, and 106), which warns against making one into two (saying 11c), and which advocates withdrawal from society (sayings 86, 27, 78, and 81).

Taking this saying seriously would lead to personal isolation from others, and in its most extreme form the saying would lead to asceticism and the anchorite life. Similar tendencies are found in other early Christian texts: 1 Cor 7:5, 7–8, 29, 32–38; Mark 8:34–37; 10:21; Luke 20:34–36. In the view of *Thomas*, a soul (sayings 25, 28, and 112) finding itself trapped in a body involved with the world (sayings 21c and 64a) would be in a wretched state indeed.

SAYING 88

Angels and prophets are coming to you. They will give you what is yours, and you also give them what you have in hand, and say to yourselves, "When are they coming to take what belongs to them?"

COMMENT

This is a very difficult saying filled with obscurities. The term "angel" (also used in saying 13) gives the saying a sense of otherworldliness: angels in the Hebrew Bible are supernatural messengers of God. But prophets are earthly messengers who speak for God; prophets also appear in early Christian texts. Individual communities had Christian prophets (1 Cor 12:10, 28–29), and there were also wandering prophets who migrated among Christian communities (see *Did.* 11–13; cf. 2, 3 John; and *Gos. Thom.* 14b). In the ancient world an angel is principally a messenger sent for some purpose (see von Rad et al., "Ἄγγελος," *TDNT*, 1.74–80). Generally in the New Testament period, angels are supernatural representatives of the heavenly world (von Rad et al., "Ἄγγελος," *TDNT*, 1.83). In one instance (Acts 12:12–15) *angel* is used as an alter-ego of Peter. In other cases, the word retains its basic idea of "messenger" or "emissary" (see Luke 7:24; 9:52; Matt 11:10; Jas 2:25). Even the term "apostle" can simply mean "emissary" (2 Cor 8:23; Phil 2:25) rather than having the technical sense Paul gives it. In *Did.* 11:3–6 *apostle* and *prophet* appear to be designations for the same function of itinerant prophetic emissary (see Plisch, *Gospel of Thomas*, 198–99): a person who brings a spiritual message from God (*Did.* 11:7—13:7). Although it is disputed, the "angels" to the seven churches of Asia (Rev 2:1, 8, 12, 18; 3:1, 7, 14) are thought by some to have been a human member of each community who served in the capacity of messenger, although in Revelation *angel* is used elsewhere for a supernatural figure.

What the spirit-inspired prophets bring is God's message for the community. What you "have in hand" and give to them is their hospitality support along the lines mentioned in *Did.* 11–13 (lodging, food, and the like.). The last sentence refers to future visits of the "messengers" and prophets of God, and "what belongs to them" is the hospitality support they expect from the community. Whether the saying is an encouragement or warning, however, is not clear. See 3 John 7–12 and 2 John 5–10.

For the Thomasine community, see saying 39a. For early Christian prophets, see Hedrick, *When History and Faith Collide*, 126–34.

SAYING 89

Why do you wash the outside of the cup? Don't you understand that the maker of the inside also made the outside?

COMMENT

The Q parallel to this saying (Luke 11:40 = Matt 23:26) is part of a series of censures of the scribes and/or Pharisees (Matt 23:13–35; Luke 11:37–44) because of their lack of inner righteousness, which is concealed by a pious outward manifestation of religion (including ritual practice; see Mark 7:2–5). The *Thomas* saying, however, has no narrative context to facilitate an interpretation. If the subject of the *Thomas* saying is simply hygienic practices, the question in the first sentence makes little sense; for who would wash only the outside of a cup and not the inside, which is the principal surface of kitchen utensils normally used? The question assumes, however, that people are doing precisely that. The second question ridicules such a practice: people who do such a thing lack understanding about the nature of hygiene. That potters made cups with both an inside and an outside, and both have to be washed, seems to be the force of the sentence. The rhetorical questions make perfect sense, however, as a condemnation of a ritual practice that fails to correct the real human failing, which has to do with the spiritual dimension that lies within (saying 6a). Superficial ritual does nothing to shape the inner person.

On the rejection of ritual in *Thomas*, see sayings 6a, 14a, and 53. On "inside" and "outside," see sayings 3a, 14c, and 22. For a discussion of rabbinic purity traditions and parallels, see DeConick, *Original Gospel of Thomas*, 256–58.

Translation and Commentary

SAYING 90

Come to me, for my yoke is kind, my lordship gentle, and you will find repose.

COMMENT

This is the only direct personal appeal Jesus makes in *Thomas* specifically for people to follow him. There are other appeals to seek (sayings 2, 76b, 92, 94), oblique encouragement to become disciples (saying 19b), an appeal to take up the cross as he did (saying 55), an appeal to give him what is his (saying 100), an offer of mystical union with him (saying 108); but saying 90 is the only direct personal appeal in *Thomas* to follow Jesus. The saying is paralleled by parts of Matt 11:28 ("come to me" and "rest"), 11:29 ("I am gentle"), and 11:30 ("my yoke is easy"). There is a parallel to Matt 11:28–30 in the third- or fourth-century *Pistis Sophia* (book 2: chap. 95). In the early gospel literature, it is clear that Jesus makes direct personal appeals for people to follow him (for example, Mark 1:17; 2:14; 10:21; Q [Matt 8:22 = Luke 9:59]; John 1:39, 43; 21:19, 22). The Thomasine community likely thought of itself as made up of "Jesus followers" in some sense. Vestiges of such an attitude are preserved in other early Christian texts (1 Cor 11:1; 1 Thess 1:6; 1 Pet 2:21; Rev 14:4). What Jesus offered to those who answered his appeal was a kind (easy) yoke (a symbol of subjection), which in the Thomasine community likely should be thought of in terms of the lax ritual obligations of the community (saying 6a).

For "repose"/"rest," see the discussion of sayings 50 and 51. See Sir 51:26–27 for "yoke" and "rest."

SAYING 91

They said to him, "Tell us who you are so we may believe in you."

He replied, "You judge the appearance of the sky and earth; yet you have not recognized who is in front of you, and don't know how to judge this opportune moment."

COMMENT

The interlocutors are not identified in *Thomas*. Matthew uses a Q saying, which parallels saying 91 (Luke 12:56 = Matt 16:3b) to chide the Pharisees and Sadducees (Matt 16:1), and in Luke Jesus addresses the saying to the multitudes. If the interlocutors are the disciples, such a statement would not be unusual in *Thomas*, since they are portrayed as making similar unperceptive statements (saying 22; see in particular saying 43). Likely, however, the saying reflects one of the few appearances where a nondisciple is given a speaking role in *Thomas* (sayings 72, 74, 79a, and 104). Other sayings in *Thomas* where Jesus is asked about his identity are 43 and 61b. Other sayings that address the recognition of Jesus are 13, 28, 37, and 52.

For the phrase "who is in front of you," see sayings 5 and 52. "Judging the appearance of sky and earth" refers either to predicting the weather, as Matt 16:2–3 and Luke 12:54–56 understand the saying, or to reading signs, omens, and portents in nature to discern the guidance of the gods (see Cicero *On Divination*: Falconer, *De senectute, De amicita, De divitione*, 214–568). "Judging this opportune moment" means recognizing the opportunity of this moment because of who Jesus is (see Eph 5:15–16). The situation is like that of the woman at the well in John 4:10. The auditors miss the opportune moment by ignoring the son of the One-Who-Lives (*Gos. Thom.* 37), who stands before them. See the Introduction for a discussion of the identity and work of Jesus in *Thomas*.

SAYING 92

Seek, and you will find. But what you previously asked me about I did not tell you at that time. Now I want to tell you, and you do not seek them.

COMMENT

The first part of this saying ("seek, and you will find") has a general parallel (Luke 11:9 = Matt 7:7) in a Q saying (Luke 11:9–13 = Matt 7:7–11). The Q saying also repeats the statement, making the same point with different words: ask, and it will be given; knock, and it will be opened.

The promise of the *Thomas* statement is that one who seeks will be rewarded by discovering that which they sought (see saying 94). The second half of the *Thomas* saying, however, portrays Jesus, the revelation bringer in *Thomas* (sayings 17, 38, 61b, 62a, 108), as refusing to honor the promise of the first statement; that is, those addressed had inquired, but Jesus did not tell them. Now, however, Jesus wants to tell them, but they no longer inquire. The discrepancy between the promise of finding and Jesus's refusal to disclose is answered in two ways. In the radical Christian tradition, the risen Lord brings new revelation after the resurrection (Gärtner, *Theology*, 117). In a mystery-religions context, disclosures are made only after a thorough grounding in the basics of the mystery. So all questions of an initiate would not be answered at first but disclosed only as progress is made in attaining higher levels of knowledge (see Clement *Letter to Theodore*, in Brown, *Mark's Other Gospel*, folio 1:17–18; folio 1:21–23; folio 2:2; *Corp herm.* 14:1). A similar lack of full disclosure on the part of Jesus is found in John 16:4b–5, 12–13. For a forthcoming attitude on the part of Jesus, see John 14:13–14; 15:7; 16:24. Mark 4:10–12 reflects a similar secrecy motif: Jesus deliberately conceals the "secret" (Mark 4:11) of the parables from the multitudes. First Corinthians 8 and Romans 14 reflect a situation of differing degrees of "knowledge" about ethical behavior in the Corinthian and Roman communities. First Corinthians 2:1–3:4 reflects differing levels of religious understanding in the community and the necessity of adjusting explanations to fit the audience (1 Cor 3:1–4). *Thomas*, saying 2, requires a diligent seeking. In

Unlocking the Secrets of the *Gospel according to Thomas*

Thomas the disciples generally ask the wrong questions (saying 22), and Jesus is portrayed as the teacher of his own mysteries (saying 62a).

SAYING 93

Do not give what is holy to dogs,
  lest they throw them on the dung pile.
Do not cast pearls to swine,
  lest they [. . .].

COMMENT

None of the suggestions to restore the lacuna are completely satisfactory (see Plisch, *Gospel of Thomas*, 207; Layton, *Nag Hammadi*, 87). There is no introductory "Jesus said" to this saying, but the original editors of the text treated it as an independent saying, and that practice has continued. In Coptic "what is holy" is singular, but "them," which is apposite to "what is holy," is plural; the two do not agree in number and should. Most translations mask the problem of how to translate the saying; as it appears above, "what" is singular.

  The Matthean parallel (Matt 7:6) does not cast the saying in a balanced synonymous parallel, as it appears in *Thomas*. The *Thomas* saying, however, lacks realism. Dogs do not throw things on dung piles, and swine do not act similarly with pearls. Perhaps "dogs" and "swine" are metaphorical abusive terms for persons who can be conceived as acting in such a manner, or for a competitor community. In the Matthean parallel, however, dogs and swine act realistically; they treat the sacred and items of high human value with complete disregard. The Matthean saying is usually conceived as symbolical or metaphorical (see Funk et al., *Five Gospels*, 154–55), but the *Thomas* saying appears to be allegory. In *Thomas*, dogs and swine are those who have no regard for the message of the community (see sayings 39a and 33a). A list of parallels can be found in DeConick, *Original Gospel of Thomas*, 265. Plisch (*Thomas*, 209), citing the study of von Lips, suggests that the saying is a "very common proverb."

SAYING 94

Whoever seeks will find [and] to [whomever knocks] will it be opened.

COMMENT

As with saying 92, the parallel here to the Q saying is only partial (Luke 11:9 = Matt 7:7). There are several sayings in *Thomas* that reflect the same sentiment of disclosure or the revealing of hidden things. Two of these place conditions on the disclosing (sayings 5 and 108), and two do not have conditions (sayings 6b and 17). In none of these instances is the content of the revelation specified—which fits *Thomas*'s invitation to seek diligently (sayings 1 and 2). See the list of early interpretations of the saying in Grant and Schoedel, *Secret Sayings of Jesus*, 180.

Translation and Commentary

SAYING 95

If you have money, don't put it out at interest, but give [it] to someone from whom you will receive nothing.

COMMENT

"Money" is singular, but the Coptic pronominal suffix to the verb "to put out" is plural. The two do not agree in number and should. The saying recommends liberal giving with no thought of receiving anything in return and specifically forbids loaning money at interest. Luke 6:34–35 makes a similar point (see also Luke 6:30 = Matt 5:42; Mark 10:21 = Matt 19:21 = Luke 18:22; Luke 12:33). The concept of liberal giving was practiced in the early Christian communities: Rom 12:8; Eph 4:28; 2 Cor 9:5–7. In Jesus's parable of the talents, however, the master of the house condemns the actions of the slave who did nothing with the money placed in his care, asserting that he should have given it to the bankers to draw interest (Luke 19:23 = Matt 25:27). See saying 109, where the rich man who became a farmer ends by becoming a moneylender, with no criticism from the *Thomas* narrator. In the Israelite tradition it was forbidden to lend money to a fellow Israelite for usury, but money may be lent to a non-Israelite at interest: see Exod 22:25; Deut 23:19–20; Lev 25:35–37. It is unclear, however, whether saying 95 is recommending liberal charity in giving or is condemning usury because it involves an engagement with the world (see sayings 21c, 64a and 64b). But it is clear that saying 14a condemns charity giving, i.e., the giving of alms. Hence saying 95 should likely be read in the context of disengagement with the world.

The saying is unusual in *Thomas* if its purpose is to recommend disinterested ethical behavior. Only two other sayings make such a recommendation: 6a ("do not lie") and 69b (go hungry to feed others). Saying 25 recommends, "love your brother" (which is a community ethic, and beneficial to those who practice it in community). The early Christian tradition, however, recommends a disinterested ethical behavior; i.e., where behavior towards others is not based on benefits that will accrue to those comporting themselves in that way: Luke 6:30 = Matt 5:42; Matt 5:23–24; Matt 5:44 = Luke 6:27; Matt 22:39 = Luke 12:31; Mark 9:35; Luke 22:25–27; Matt 19:21 = Mark 10:21; Matt 26:9 = Mark 14:5; John

12:5; 13:29; Rom 12:17, 20–21; Jas 2:1–5; *Did.* 1:5–6 (see the discussion in Plisch, *Gospel of Thomas*, 211 for further parallels). *Thomas*, however, is concerned primarily with inner spirituality and disengagement from the world.

SAYING 96

The Father's imperial rule is like [a] woman, who took a little leaven, [concealed] it in dough, and made large bread loaves. Whoever has ears had better pay attention.

COMMENT

The Q parallel to this saying (Luke 13:20–21 = Matt 13:33) is different from the *Thomas* version in several significant features. The Q story begins with the leaven; Thomas begins with the woman. Nevertheless, parable scholars understand the comparison in Jesus's stories to lie between the imperial rule and the story as a whole (Jeremias, *Parables of Jesus*, 101–2). *Thomas* stresses the small amount of leaven ("a little"), and the Q story stresses the large amount of flour (3 measures equals a little over a bushel of flour). Hence *Thomas* makes a contrast between small leaven and multiple large loaves (or possibly few and many; see sayings 8 and 20). Q makes a contrast between leaven (normally small, but here the amount is not stated) and a large bushel of flour that was leavened (see sayings 8 and 20). Leaven is a negative concept in the Bible (Scott, *Hear Then the Parable*, 324–25; for example, Mark 8:15; 1 Cor 5:6–8; Gal 5:7–10), but in *Thomas* (and in the Q parable) it is used positively—a scandalous use of a negative concept for a positive reason.

Because many things happen in a parable or story, multiple applications may be drawn from it. A reader, however, may abstract this story in *Thomas* as follows: The force concealed within is a mighty transforming power. In *Thomas* the transforming force is the inner presence of the divine; see sayings 3b, 11c, 22, 50, 70, 106, and 108.

For the relationship of imperial rule and the self-originating light, see sayings 49 (the elect will find the kingdom because they are from it) and 50 (the elect have come from the self-originated light). On the inner quality of the imperial rule, see saying 3a. For a discussion of parables, see sayings 9, 20, 21a, 57, and 63. For "better pay attention to this," see saying 8.

SAYING 97

The [Father's] imperial rule is like a woman carrying a [jar] full of meal. While she was walking [on a] road some distance (from home), the handle of the jar broke, and the meal spilled behind her [on] the road. She was unaware and did not know of the problem. After reaching her house, she put the jar down and found it empty.

COMMENT

No parallels exist to this story. The comparison lies between the Father's imperial rule and the story as a whole (see saying 96). A woman is returning home with a jar of ground meal. While she was still a long way from home, the handle breaks and the meal spills out behind her. She is completely oblivious to this unexpected turn of events, and upon arriving home discovers that her previously full jar is empty. In *Thomas* the story warns the reader against the dangers (saying 21b) and uncertainties (saying 63) of involvement with the world (saying 64a). This is how it is under the Father's imperial rule; you can go from "full" to "empty" in an instant by being unaware of the dangers you face. So the spiritual person will be perceptive (saying 21d) and always watchful (saying 21b). Other sayings in *Thomas* that stress similar warnings against ignorance of one's risk in the world are 28, 91, and 109. Similar cautions are found in other early Christian literature: for instance, 1 John 2:16; 2 Tim 4:10; Mark 4:14–19; Luke 21:34; Heb 3:12–14; 2 Pet 2:20–22; Eph 6:11–18; 1 Pet 5:8–9. See the cautious reading of this story in Davies, *Gospel of Thomas*, 118.

SAYING 98

The Father's imperial rule is like a person wanting to kill a nobleman. Drawing the sword in his house, he thrust it into the wall to test the strength of his hand, and then killed the nobleman.

COMMENT

There are no other versions of this story in early Christian literature. Although stories attributed to Jesus generally deal with flawed characters, this story of a cold-blooded murder is the most problematic in the entire parables corpus (Hedrick, "Survivors of the Crucifixion," 174–76; and Hedrick, "Flawed Heroes and Stories Jesus Told"). Several commentators have called attention to the twin stories of the tower builder and of the king going forth to war (Luke 14:28–32) as similar stories that make an admonition to "thorough preparation before action." Sayings in *Thomas* cited as parallels to this way of evaluating saying 98 are 10, 16a, and 35 (Davies, *Gospel of Thomas*, 110). But it appears that the protagonist in this story goes from concept to accomplishment with no reasonable planning or forethought, which is exactly the opposite of the stories in Luke. If a prudent person will always look before leaping, the protagonist in this story leaps without looking and is completely successful (Hedrick, "Flawed Heroes and the Stories Jesus Told"). The victim is a nobleman, a leading figure of the land; see Mark 6:21; Rev 16:15; *Gos. Thom.* 78). The story may be abstracted as advocating bold action even when there is great personal risk. In terms of the imperial rule of God, the story advocates taking bold action to ensure that one finds or enters the imperial realm, even if that action flies in the face of common wisdom (saying 8) or makes one appear less than prudent (saying 76a). Other parables not in *Thomas* seem to have the same general thrust: for example, Matt 13:44; 13:45–46; Luke 15:4–6; (*Gos. Thom.* 107); Luke 16:1–7. Other sayings in *Thomas* suggesting bold action are 4a, 8, and 36. See Sir 8:1–3; 4:7, which recognize the risky business of going against powerful community leaders.

SAYING 99

The disciples said to him, "Your brothers and your mother are standing outside."

He replied, "Those hereabouts doing my Father's will are my brothers and my mother. They will enter into my Father's imperial rule."

COMMENT

There is a longer parallel to this saying in the Synoptic Gospels: Mark 3:31–35 = Matt 12:47–50 = Luke 8:19–21. The closest parallel, however, is with Luke 8:20–21. In the Synoptic Gospels the statement about his mother's and his brothers' being outside (in a different order than *Thomas*) is made by persons other than the disciples. In all texts his mother and brothers are described as "standing outside." "Sisters" are only mentioned by Matthew and *Gospel of the Ebionites* (Miller, *Complete Gospels*, fragment 5). In Matthew (12:49) Jesus indicates that his disciples are his family (i.e., his mother and his brothers). And all texts have a more universal response as well: "My mother and my brothers are those do the will of God/Father" (Luke: "who hear the word of God and do it"). In all texts Jesus's natural family members are not included as his "family" but are left "outside." Matthew and *2 Clem.* 9:11 (which only cites "brothers") read, "the will of my Father."

Thomas, like the Synoptic Gospels, replaces the primary family circle with the religious community and ties their relationship to doing God's will ("those hereabouts doing my Father's will"). In the religious community, there is a higher-order relationship superseding the natural family unit. This is the only *Thomas* saying dealing with the will of the Father, but saying 79a promises a blessing to those who hear and keep the word of God. See also sayings 16b, 55, 101, and 105.

SAYING 100

They showed Jesus a gold coin and said, "Caesar's people demand taxes from us."
  He replied, "Give to Caesar what is his and to God what belongs to him, and what is mine, give to me."

COMMENT

The narrative parallel in the Synoptic Gospels (Mark 12:13–17 = Matt 22:15–22 = Luke 20:20–26) is extensive. In *Thomas* the interlocutors are anonymous but are identified in the Synoptic Gospels. In the Synoptic Gospels they bring the coin to Jesus at his request, but in *Thomas* an unspecific "they" initiates Jesus's response by presenting the coin to him. The final pronouncement of Jesus is identical in both the Synoptic Gospels and *Thomas*, except that in *Thomas* Jesus adds that he be given what is due him as well.

The remarkable thing about the saying is its ambiguity. The content of what is due to each of the parties mentioned in the saying is unspecified. Many of Jesus's sayings are ambiguous, prompting the question; so what am I supposed to do—specifically? Compare Mark 10:25; Matt 10:16; Matt 19:12; Luke 6:20; and *Gos. Thom.* 69b. And of course the most oblique of all Jesus's sayings are the parables. For further parallels, see DeConick, *Original Gospel of Thomas*, 276–77. See *Gos. Thom.* 77a and 77b, where Jesus encroaches on the traditional role of the Father. In saying 100 Jesus at the very least makes himself equal with the Father, and—it might be added—also with Caesar.

SAYING 101

Whoever does not hate [father] and mother as I do will be unable to be my [disciple], and whoever does [not] love [father and] mother as I do will be unable to be my [disciple], for my mother [. . . .], but [my] true [mother] gave me life.

COMMENT

The first part of this saying (with regard to hating parents) is partially paralleled in saying 55 and Luke 14:26. Another parallel exists in Matt 10:37 relative to loving parents more than Jesus.

Saying 55 is hyperbole commending single-minded devotion in discipleship. Saying 101, on the other hand, is an antithetical parallelism and a paradox (i.e., a self-contradictory statement). How is it possible truly to hate and love parents at the same time? Matthew 10:16b is a similar paradox: how is it possible to be "sly like snakes and simple as pigeons" at one and the same time (see the discussion in Hedrick, *Many Things in Parables*, vii–ix)? Several suggestions have been made for restoring the lacuna in the last part of the saying, but there is no consensus. Jesus's mother is referred to as the Holy Spirit in *Gos. Heb.* fragments 4a, 4b, and 4c (Miller, *Complete Gospels*, 431–33); *Ap. Jas.* 6:19–20. A resolution of the paradox suggested by some is that the first parents mentioned in the antithetical parallel, who are to be hated, are the biological parents, and the second, who are to be loved, are the spiritual parents (see the discussion in Plisch, *Gospel of Thomas*, 220–23). If this is the case, the paradox recommends single-minded devotion to the spiritual parents. See also saying 105.

SAYING 102

Shame on the Pharisees, for they are like a dog lying asleep in the oxen's feeding trough: it neither eats nor [allows] the oxen to eat.

COMMENT

The same sentiment about the Pharisees is expressed in saying 39a and Matt 23:13 (cf. Luke 11:52). Saying 102 is an abbreviated version of a fable attributed to Aesop (see Perry, *Babrius and Phaedrus*: "The Dog in the Manger," fable 702, p. 597; for other parallels, see Stroker, *Extracanonical Sayings*, 148–49). Woes against the Pharisees are found in the canonical tradition (Luke 11:42–43; Matt 23:13–15, 23, 25, 27, 29). "Shame," see Hanson, "'How Honorable!' 'How Shameful!'" He argues that makarisms and woes should be understood in terms of the honor/shame value system of the ancient Mediterranean world.

As in saying 39a, the Pharisees are censured for blocking access to spiritual enlightenment (i.e., the imperial rule) on the part of those seeking it. Most probably a rival religious community (saying 39a) is the target of the censure, if not the Jewish community itself, since a Jewish community had existed in Alexandria from the earliest period.

SAYING 103

Whoever knows where thieves will strike are favored. They can get up, bring together the [. . . .], and prepare for action before the break-in.

COMMENT

Two possibilities for restoring the word lost in lacuna are as follows: one is to restore T̄M̄NTE2O as an abstract noun, "treasure" (i.e., what is regarded as valuable); a second, restored by several scholars T̄M̄NTEPO as an abstract noun meaning "domain" (i.e., estate) or "dominion" (i.e., persons under the homeowner's sphere of influence). Saying 21b is a near duplicate of this saying, or at least expresses the same sentiments.

"Favored," see saying 19a. The spiritual person will be perceptive and prepare for the dangers that involvement with the world brings (see sayings 21c, 64a, 64b, and 97; Mark 3:27). The image of a thief in the night is used in early Christianity to prepare for the day of the Lord: 1 Thess 5:2; 2 Pet 3:10; Rev 3:3; 16:14–15. "Prepare for action" reads literally "gird up your loins." "Before the break-in" reads literally "before they come in."

SAYING 104

They said [to him], "Come and pray today, and fast."
　　Jesus replied, "Why, what sin have I done, or what has mastered me? But let people fast and pray when the bridegroom leaves the wedding chamber."

COMMENT

Fasting and prayer are negative behaviors in *Thomas* (saying 6a), so naturally Jesus declines to fast and pray, for fasting is sinful, and praying brings condemnation (saying 14a). The Thomasine community practiced "fasting from the world" (saying 27). The anonymous interlocutors (disciples? Pharisees? community rivals [cf. saying 39a]?), however, clearly seem to approve of such behaviors. Jesus's response suggests that the only reason people might pray or fast is that they have committed sin or caved in to negative influences that have gained control of their lives so that the sinners need to perform penitence. Jesus has done neither.

　　The cryptic response about the bridegroom is puzzling. Is Jesus the bridegroom, or is he referring to another figure? In Luke 5:33–35 Jesus explains why he and his disciples are not praying and fasting (only fasting in Matt 9:14–15 and Mark 2:18–20) by making an analogy between, on the one hand, himself and his circle of disciples, and, on the other hand, what occurs in a marriage celebration. The identity of the bridegroom in Luke 5:35 seems to be a direct reference to Jesus, and the "taking away" of the bridegroom is an allusion to the crucifixion, an event leading the disciples to fast and pray. In *Thomas*, people fast and pray only when the bridegroom leaves the wedding chamber. Matthew unambiguously makes the identification clear that Jesus is the bridegroom in the interpretation (Matt 25:13) of the story of the ten maidens (Matt 25:1–13). See the discussion in saying 75 of the bridegroom and wedding chamber. In *Thomas* there is no indication of events occurring in the wedding chamber (saying 75). In Valentinianism, however, the bridal chamber corrects the deficiency caused to the first human at creation (*Gos. Phil.* 70:9–22). Adam was first created as an androgynous (male-female) being (Gen 2:7) but lost the female principle when Eve was formed from his rib (Gen 2:18–23). Male and female thus became a single gender again in the bridal chamber. Valentinians believed that evil spirits are either male or female, and they attack human souls. Male spirits mingle with the female human soul, defiling it; and in like manner female spirits defile the male human soul. In the imaged bridal chamber an "image" unites with an "angel" and through the union human souls are immune to evil spirits (*Gos. Phil.* 65:1–26). Jesus denies that he has sinned in the *Gospel of the Nazoreans* (or the *Gospel of the Hebrews*: Miller, *Complete Gospels*, fragment 2, pages 431, 443). Some early followers of Jesus practiced times of prayer and fasting: *Did.* 8:1–3; 1 Cor 7:5; Acts 2:42; 10:30; 13:2–3; 14:23.

SAYING 105

Whoever would know father and mother will be called the whore's child.

COMMENT

Here "know" is in the sense of "acknowledge." See sayings 55 and 101, where biological parentage is rejected, perhaps in favor of a spiritual parentage. That people who acknowledge relationships with biological parents are not single-minded in their relationship to the living Father characterizes the attitude of this cluster of sayings. Such people are whore's children in the sense that they have no spiritual father and mother as Jesus does (saying 101). The saying plays off the idea that children born of copulation with a prostitute have no father who claims them. They do not know their father and hence are "illegitimate" (see John 8:39–41; Heb 12:8; Hos 2:4–5; cf. *Gos. Phil.* 52:21–24). Because their biological mothers cannot reveal their true (spiritual) heritage, they are prostitutes, and therefore their children are whores' children (see saying 101: "my [true] mother gives life").

SAYING 106

When you make the two one, you will become Adam's children, and when you say, "Mountain, move over," it will move."

COMMENT

See the discussion of the doublet of this saying in saying 48. "Adam's children" (see saying 86 for "son of Adam") are those who will become children of the original human being before his devolution into separate genders, by reducing the two genders to one (see sayings 104 and 114). In the discussion of saying 28, on the other hand, "humanity's children" are descendents of Adam after his separation into the male and female genders. The imperial rule is characterized by singularity, however, and once the two become one, they are the solitary who have found the imperial rule (saying 49).

For "Adam," see sayings 85 and 86. For "making the two one," see saying 22.

SAYING 107

The imperial rule is like a shepherd having one hundred sheep. One of them, the large one, strayed. He abandoned the ninety-nine and sought after the single (stray) until it was found. After the difficult (search), he told the sheep, "I love you more than the ninety-nine."

COMMENT

The *Thomas* parable has a parallel in Q: Matt 18:12–13 = Luke 15:4. Luke has expanded the story by adding a second movement (15:5–6), which is not paralleled in Matthew and *Thomas*. By comparing the Q material to *Thomas*'s story, one observes that the *Thomas* story concerns straying and finding. Matthew's story, on the other hand, is about straying, finding, and rejoicing, while Luke's story is about losing, finding, rejoicing; and (with Luke's second movement added) Luke also is concerned with celebrating. In Matthew and *Thomas* the sheep *strays*, but in Luke the sheep is *lost*. Matthew and Luke emphasize the dangers to the strayed or lost sheep by noting the dangerous locations where the sheep strayed or was lost. *Thomas* alone notes the difficulty of the search and gives a motive for leaving the ninety-nine behind: i.e., the shepherd's love for the "one." Common sense says that ninety-nine sheep are worth more than one, single sheep, no matter how large. Nevertheless, all three versions of the story focus on the one and ignore the ninety-nine. (On other parables in *Thomas*, see sayings 9, 20, and 96–98.) In *Thomas*'s view, spiritual insight is always superior to common wisdom, and hence the shepherd selects the "one" (sayings 76a and 4a) over the "many" (sayings 8 and 4b).

On the One, see sayings 37 and 50. A similar emphasis on the "one"—on singularity and unity—is found among early followers of Jesus with respect to the divine (Mark 12:29–30; John 10:30; 17:21; Rom 3:30; 1 Cor 8:4–6; Gal 3:20; 1 Tim 2:5; cf. Deut 6:4), with respect to the individual (1 Cor 6:16–17; Eph 6:5; Col 3:22; Matt 6:22–23 = Luke 11:34), and with respect to the community (John 10:16; 17:20–23; Rom 12:5; 1 Cor 3:8; 10:17; 12:12–13, 20; Gal 3:28; Eph 2:14–15; Phil 1:27; Acts 4:32; cf. Jer 32:39; Ezek 11:19; Zech 14:9; Mal 2:10, 15). Diversity within the individual is a negative: Jas 1:8; 4:8; Ps 12:2.

Unlocking the Secrets of the *Gospel according to Thomas*

Note the different literary contexts of Matthew (18:10, 14) and Luke (15:1–3, 7) in which Matthew and Luke perform the Q parable. These contexts signal the way each writer understood the parable. See also the *Gos. Truth* NHC I,3:31:35—32:34 for a Valentinian reading of the story.

SAYING 108

Whoever will drink from my mouth will become like I am. I myself will become as he is, and what is concealed will be revealed to him.

COMMENT

This is the clearest statement in *Thomas* of the mystical character of the text. In *Thomas* the way to the living Father is by looking within (saying 3b) and making a mystical return to the One (saying 18), where one achieves a mystical union with the One (sayings 11c and 42). In saying 108, mystical union with Jesus for members of the community is part of the mystical journey into the One—not unlike Paul's mystical union with Christ: Rom 12:5; 1 Cor 6:17; 12:12–13; Gal 2:20. (See also the New Testament references mentioned in the analysis of saying 107.) Drinking from Jesus's mouth is assimilating his words (*Gos. Thom.* 1; Sir 24:21; see also Prov 8:5–8; 10:31; Exod 4:15; Ps 37:30; 49:3) or another metaphor used in *Thomas* having the same idea: drinking from the bubbling spring (*Gos. Thom.* 13; John 4:13–14; 7:37–38). The experience brings about the assimilation into the divine. See the parallels from the *Odes of Solomon* in Gärtner, *Theology*, 131–34. Since the default gender for the solitaries is male (see sayings 114, 49), it is unclear whether the use of the Coptic masculine pronouns in this saying are due to the lack of an inclusive pronoun in Coptic or by design.

For concealed things being revealed, see the discussion of sayings 5, 6b, 17, and 94. On two becoming one, see sayings 4b, 22, and 106.

SAYING 109

The imperial rule is like a person having a [hidden] treasure in his field, [but] is unaware of it. [Before] he died, the deceased man left it (the field) to his [son]. The son, also [unaware], sold the field, and the new owner plowed and [found] the treasure. He began to lend at interest to [whomever] he wanted.

COMMENT

Matthew's hidden-treasure story (Matt 13:44) is quite different from the version in *Thomas*. *Thomas*'s version is a short paragraph parable, but Matthew's version is a sentence parable (a third type is a multiple-paragraphs parable: see Hedrick, "Survivors of the Crucifixion," 168–69). Matthew's version has a single focus (one owner), but *Thomas*'s version has a multiple focus (three owners). "[Before] he died": this lacuna is usually restored as M̄[M̄N̄NCA T]ΡЄϥΜΟΥ: "after he died," which is too short for the lacuna. I have restored it two letters longer as M̄[ΠΑΤϥΜΟΥ Π]ΡЄϥΜΟΥ: "before he died," to accommodate the logical problem that the father could do nothing after he was dead.

Apparently neither the original owner nor the son who inherited the property had worked the field, since the final owner plowed and accidentally found the treasure. The final owner apparently abandons farming to become a moneylender, which violates Jesus's explicit directive not to loan money at interest (saying 95) as well as an additional cluster of sayings directing a withdrawal from society (sayings 86, 27, 78, 81, 64a, and 64b). Hence the actions of the treasure-finder are questionable in terms of *Thomas*, where those who discover the world and become rich are advised to deny the world (saying 110). This leaves the reader with the conundrum, was the life of this treasure-finder enhanced or subverted by the discovery of the treasure? That is to say, does wealth corrupt or liberate? In the context of *Thomas* it is very difficult to see this story in a positive way, even if one were to imagine, for example, that it might be understood allegorically as a search for the imperial rule. The story violates too many of the standard themes of *Thomas*. For example, saying 110 seems to contradict 109, and none of the protagonists in the *Thomas* story are actually searching for the treasure; it is found accidentally.

Thomas regularly admonishes one to seek (sayings 1, 2, 62a, 60, 76b, 92, and 94), for only then can they "find" (sayings 27 and 49); so this story also violates the seeking theme.

For other parables in *Thomas* see the list in saying 9, and the discussion under each. The parables of Jesus have no interpretations *within* the story. The synoptic evangelists provide literary contexts for the parables, and attach brief explanations at the end of the stories, both of which aid readers in understanding the parables as the evangelists did (Hedrick, *Many Things in Parables*, 10–14). The stories themselves were open-ended, leaving the "explanation" up to auditors (Funk, "Good Samaritan as Metaphor," 34). The incipit "the imperial rule is like" is not part of the story itself but an interpretive comparative frame that was not originally a part of the story (see Hedrick, "Parable and Kingdom," 193–99). There are several hidden-treasure parables in the ancient world: see Stroker, *Extracanonical Sayings*, 57–60; and Crossan, *Finding Is the First Act*.

Unlocking the Secrets of the *Gospel according to Thomas*

SAYING 110

Whoever <would> find [the] world and become rich should deny the world.

COMMENT:

"Whoever <would> find": the text reads a Coptic perfect, not a future; but the following Coptic conjunctive in the second clause cannot continue the use of the perfect in the first; the text above is emended to Coptic future, following Layton's suggested emendation (*Nag Hammadi Codex II*, 92). See the discussion under saying 109, and cf. 80 and 81.

In *Thomas*, "world" represents a construct of life directly opposed to life under the imperial rule of God (saying 21c). Everything associated with such a way of life is to be rejected (see the discussions of sayings 63, 64a, 64b, 28, 29, and 56). See the parallels to this saying in DeConick, *Original Gospel of Thomas*, 291.

SAYING 111

The heavens and the earth will roll up in front of you; yet one who lives out of the One-Who-Lives will not see death—not to mention that Jesus says, "Find yourself and the world is unworthy of you."

COMMENT

See the discussion of saying 11a. This saying sets up a contrast between the obsolescence of the physical universe (however conceived) and the state of those who have grounded their being in the One-Who-Lives by having discovered themselves (saying 3b). Discovering oneself brings union with the divine (saying 3b) and results in immortality. The cosmos was created as the dominion of Adam (Gen 1:26–30). And it was good (Gen 1:31)—one might say it was worthy of God's creatures. Nevertheless, the world is unworthy of those who discover themselves (sayings 56 and 80). They are from the One-Who-Lives (saying 50) and will "go there again" (sayings 49 and 18); their destination is not a place located in the cosmic realm. It is spiritually located. *Thomas* rejects the renewed-creation concept of Paul (Rom 8:18–23) and Rev 21:1–4; the Thomasine vision is more like the spiritual vision of the Gospel of John (14:1–7; 17:14–16, 24).

For "roll up of the heavens and earth," see Isa 34:4; Rev 6:14; Heb 1:12; *Pistis Sophia*, book 1: chap. 3 (MacDermot, *Pistis Sophia*, 12–13). On "not to mention that Jesus says," see Goodwin, *A Greek Grammar*, section 1504; and Plisch, *Gospel of Thomas*, 112, n. 5. The last phrase has all the earmarks of a later addition to saying 111. Jesus would not have said "not to mention that Jesus says," but rather he would have said, "not to mention that I say." I have treated the last phrase here as an addition rather than as an independent saying. See the discussion in Valantasis, *Gospel of Thomas*, 190–92.

SAYING 112

Shameful the flesh,
  hanging on the soul;
shameful the soul,
  hanging on the flesh!

COMMENT

"Shameful," see saying 102. The flesh and the soul/spirit are not concordant with one another, but are actually discordant (see sayings 87, 29). Saying 112 describes in a poetic way that conflicted and tenuous relationship as "hanging"; that is, the two are not an integrated whole but incompatible with one another. Compare the Valentinian hymn "Summer Harvest": "Flesh hanging from soul" (Layton, *Gnostic Scriptures*, 246–48). *Thomas* does not subscribe to the Hebrew concept that a human being is a "living being" (see saying 29)—that is, an integrated whole (Gen 2:7). Rather, *Thomas*'s dualistic view that human beings are a conflicted tension of body or flesh and spirit or soul (see saying 29) is more akin to the Greek concept that a human being is composed of body, soul, and spirit (see the brief discussion in Koester, *History, Culture, and Religion*, 139–40). In *Thomas*'s view, both body/flesh and spirit/soul are condemned. The spirit, however, is that great "wealth," inhabiting somatic poverty (saying 29) that is assured of immortality by a person rightly understanding the words of Jesus (sayings 1 and 2). Certain passages from early Christian texts suggest a tendency among the early followers of Jesus to think of the spirit/soul and body/flesh dualistically: Matt 10:28; Rom 8:9–11; 1 Cor 5:5; Gal 5:17; 1 Thess 5:23; Heb 4:12; Jas 1:21; 4:5; 5:20; 1 Pet 1:9; 2:11; *1 Clem.* 49:6; *2 Clem.* 5:4–5; 9:1–4; 12:2–4; *Barn.* 21:8.

SAYING 113

His disciples asked, "When will the imperial rule come?"
"It will not come by looking for it. No one is going to say, 'Look, here it is,' or 'see, there it is.' But the Father's imperial rule is spread out on the earth; yet people do not see it."

COMMENT

Once again the disciples show their lack of insight (see the discussion under sayings 22 and 51) in not perceiving the presence of the imperial rule. Jesus contradicts them; the imperial rule of the Father is not a "thing" to be observed with the eye; rather, it is a pervasive spiritual reality. See the parallel in Luke 17:20-21 (cf. Mark 13:21; Matt 24:23, 26-27; Luke 17:23-24), and the discussion of saying 3a. A similar idea appears in *Gos. Mary* 8:12-19. *Thomas* is aware of a cosmic apocalyptic expectation of the end of the cosmos (see sayings 111 and 11a) but does not associate that event with the coming or presence of the imperial rule. In this respect *Thomas* shares the dominant view of the imperial rule in the Gospel of John. The dominant eschatology of the Gospel of John is a realized eschatology (John 3:16-21; 3:36; 4:14; 5:21, 24-25; 11:24-26; 12:31). The future cosmic expectation is barely represented in John (6:39-40, 44b, 54; 12:48) but is a major aspect of early Christian belief (for example, Mark 13; and 1 Cor 7:17-31). On futuristic eschatology and realized eschatology, see the summary in Perrin, *Kingdom of God*, 58-78.

SAYING 114

Simon Peter said to them, "Let's put Mary out of our group, for women are not worthy of life."
    Jesus replied, "Look here, I myself will lead her to make her male, so that even she may become a live spirit, like you males; for every female making herself male will come under the imperial rule of heaven."

COMMENT

"Lead her": it is unclear what Jesus will do to make her male, or how she will "make herself male." The background of the saying is the necessity of returning to the original state of the first human being. Adam was created as a living soul (Gen 2:7), who contained within himself both the male and the female principle (Gen 2:21–23). When Eve was separated from Adam, it was seen as an aberration of the original state of creation (*Apoc. Adam* 64:20–28). Only those who regain the original androgynous union of the first human being are worthy of life. Priority in this saying is given to the male principle (Gen 2:7), however, even though the first human being was neither male nor female but rather both male and female, an androgynous whole. See a similar attitude on the part of Paul in 1 Cor 11:7–12.

The background of saying 114 is presumed by several other sayings in *Thomas*; see the discussion of sayings 11c, 104, 106, and also 28, 29, 37, and 43. Peter's statement seems to assume that women are completely excluded from the imperial rule. The response of Jesus, on the other hand, appears to be a gentle reprimand to Peter, for women too can become male-female. Apparently the disciples are again making a wrong assumption (see saying 22) in thinking that only males are worthy of life. At this point none of them have yet become solitaries, however, and only the solitaries will achieve that original primordial union of creation (see *Gos. Phil.* 68:22–26; 70:9–22).

On "rule of heaven," see saying 3b. On "become a live spirit," cf. 1 Cor 6:17. See Hippolytus *Ref.* 5.8.44: "all become bridegrooms, having been made male through the virgin spirit" (Meyer, *Gospel of Thomas*, 109); and Clement *Exc.* 21.3: "The female, having become male, unites itself with the angels, and enters into the Pleroma. Therefore it is said that the woman is changed into a man" (Foerster, *Gnosis*, 224).

The Gospel according to Thomas

Bibliography

Allberry, C. R. C., editor. *A Manichaean Psalm-Book, Part II*. Manichaean Manuscripts of the Chester Beatty Collection 2. Stuttgart: Kohlhammer, 1938.
Allen, R. E., translator. *Plato's Parmenides*. Rev. ed. The Dialogues of Plato 4. New Haven: Yale University Press, 1997.
Altaner, Berthold. *Patrology*. Translated by Hilda C. Graef. Freiburg: Herder & Herder, 1960.
Attridge, Harry W. "Greek Fragments." In *Nag Hammadi Codex II*, edited by Bentley Layton, 2:96–102. The Coptic Gnostic Library. NHS 20. Leiden: Brill, 1988.
Bauer, Walter. *Orthodoxy and Heresy in Earliest Christianity*. Edited by Robert A. Kraft and Gerhard Krodel. Translated by a team from the Philadelphia Seminar on Christian Origins. Philadelphia: Fortress, 1971.
Bell, H. Idris. *Cults and Creeds in Graeco-Roman Egypt*. The Forwood Lectures, 1952. Chicago: Ares, 1985.
Betz, Hans Dieter, editor. *The Greek Magical Papyri in Translation, including the Demotic Spells*. 2nd ed. Chicago: University of Chicago Press, 1992.
Brown, Raymond E. *The Gospel according to John*. 2 vols. AB 29–29A. Garden City, NY: Doubleday, 1966.
Brown, Scott G. *Mark's Other Gospel: Rethinking Morton Smith's Controversial Discovery*. Studies in Christianity and Judaism 15. Toronto: Wilfrid Laurier University Press, 2005.
Bultmann, Rudolf. *The History of the Synoptic Tradition*. Translated by John Marsh. Oxford: Blackwell, 1963.
———. *Theology of the New Testament*. 2 vols. Translated by Kendrick Grobel. New York: Scribner, 1951–1955.
Charlesworth, James A. "Paradise." In *ABD*, 5:154–55.
Connolly, R. Hugh, editor. *Didascalia Apostolorum*. Ancient Texts and Translations. 1929. Reprint, Eugene, OR: Wipf & Stock, 2010.
Copenhaver, Brian P. *Hermetica: The Greek "Corpus Hermeticum" and the Latin "Asclepius" in a New English Translation, with Notes and Introduction*. Cambridge: Cambridge University Press, 1992.
Crossan, John Dominic. *Finding Is the First Act. Trove Folktales and Jesus' Treasure Parable*. Semeia Supplements. 1979. Reprint, Eugene, OR: Wipf & Stock, 2008.
———. *In Fragments. The Aphorisms of Jesus*. 1983. Reprint, Eugene, OR: Wipf & Stock, 2008.
Dalmann, Gustaf. *Jesus-Jeshua, Studies in the Gospels*. Translated by Paul P. Levertoff. 1971. Reprint, Eugene, OR: Wipf & Stock, 2004.

Bibliography

Davies, Stevan L. *The Gospel of Thomas Annotated & Explained.* SkyLight Illuminations Series. Woodstock, VT: SkyLight Paths, 2002.

DeConick, April D., translator. *The Original Gospel of Thomas in Translation.* Library of New Testament Studies 287. Early Christianity in Context. London: T. & T. Clark, 2007.

Dodd, C. H. *The Interpretation of the Fourth Gospel.* Cambridge: Cambridge University Press, 1965.

Dodds, Erik Robertson, and John Miles Dillon. "Plotinus." In *The Oxford Classical Dictionary*, edited by Simon Hornblower and Antony Spawforth, 1198–200. 3rd ed. Oxford: Oxford University Press, 1999.

Drijvers, Han J. W. "The Acts of Thomas." In *New Testament Apocrypha*, edited by Wilhelm Schneelmelcher and R. McL. Wilson, 2:322–411. 2 vols. Rev. ed. Cambridge: James Clarke, 1991.

Eliade, Mircea. *The Myth of the Eternal Return.* Translated by Willard R. Trask. Bollingen Series 46. New York: Pantheon, 1954.

Eusebius. *The Ecclesiastical History.* Translated by Kirsopp Lake. 2 vols. LCL. London: Heinemann, 1965.

Falconer, William Armistead, translator. *Cicero: De senectute, De amicita, De divitione, with an English Translation.* LCL. Cambridge: Harvard University Press, 1959.

Ferguson, Everett. *Backgrounds of Early Christianity.* 2nd ed. Grand Rapids, Eerdmans, 1993.

Foerster, Werner. *Gnosis: A Selection of Gnostic Texts.* Vol. 1, *Patristic Evidence.* Edited by R. McL. Wilson. Oxford: Clarendon, 1972.

Freedman, David Noel, et al., editors. *The Anchor Bible Dictionary.* 6 vols. New York: Doubleday, 1992.

Funk, Robert W. "The Good Samaritan as Metaphor." In *Parables and Presence: Forms of the New Testament Tradition*, 29–34. Philadelphia: Fortress, 1982.

Funk, Robert W., Roy W. Hoover, and The Jesus Seminar. *The Five Gospels: The Search for the Authentic Words of Jesus; A New Translation and Commentary.* San Francisco: HarperSanFrancisco, 1993.

Gardner, Iain, editor. *The Kephalaia of the Teacher: The Edited Coptic Manichaean Texts in Translation with Commentary.* Nag Hammadi and Manichaean Studies 37. Leiden: Brill, 1995.

Gärtner, Bertil. *The Theology of the Gospel according to Thomas.* Translated by Eric J. Sharpe. London: Collins, 1961.

Ginzberg, Louis. *The Legends of the Jews.* Translated by Henrietta Szold. 7 vols. Philadelphia: Jewish Publication Society of America, 1968.

Goodspeed, Edgar J., and Robert M. Grant. *A History of Early Christian Literature.* Chicago: University of Chicago Press, 1966.

Goodwin, William W. *A Greek Grammar.* London: Macmillan, 1968.

Grant, Robert M., and William R. Schoedel. *The Secret Sayings of Jesus: The Gnostic Gospel of Thomas.* A Dolphin Book. Garden City, NY: Doubleday, 1960.

Grenfell, Bernard P., and Arthur S. Hunt, editors and translators. *ΛΟΓΙΑ ΙΗΣΟΥ: Sayings of Our Lord from an Early Greek Papyrus.* Published for the Egypt Exploration Society. London: Frowde, 1897.

———, editors and translators. *The Oxyrhynchus Papyri Part 1: Edited with Translations and Notes.* London: Egypt Exploration Fund, 1898.

Bibliography

———, editors and translators. *The Oxyrhynchus Papyri Part IV: Edited with Translations and Notes*. London: Egypt Exploration Fund, 1904.
Guillaumont, A., et al. *The Gospel according to Thomas: Coptic Text Established and Translated*. Leiden: Brill, 1959.
Guillaumont, A. "Les sémitismes dans l'Évangile selon Thomas: Essai de classement." In *Studies in Gnosticism and Hellenistic Religion: Presented to Gilles Quispel on the Occasion of his 65th Birthday*, edited by R. van den Broek and M. J. Vermaseren, 190–204. EPRO 91. Leiden: Brill, 1981.
Hanson, K. C. "'How Honorable!' 'How Shameful!' A Cultural Analysis of Matthew's Makarisms and Reproaches." *Semeia* 68 (1994[96]) 81–111.
Harkness, Georgia. *Mysticism: Its Meaning and Message*. Nashville: Abingdon, 1973.
Harnack, Adolf von. *Marcion: The Gospel of the Alien God*. Translated by John E. Steely and Lyle D. Bierma. Durham, NC: Labyrinth, 1990.
Hedrick, Charles W. "An Anecdotal Argument for the Independence of the *Gospel of Thomas* from the Synoptic Gospels." In *For the Children, Perfect Instruction: Studies in Honor of Hans-Martin Schenke on the Occasion of the Berliner Arbeitskreis für koptisch-gnostische Schriften's Thirtieth Year*, edited by Hans-Gephardt Bethge, et al., 113–26. Nag Hammadi and Manichaean Studies 54. Leiden: Brill, 2002.
———. "Flawed Heroes and Stories Jesus Told: The One about a Killer." In *The Handbook for the Study of the Historical Jesus*. Edited by T. Holmén and S. E. Porter, 4.3021–3054. 4 vols. Leiden: Brill, 2010.
———. *Many Things in Parables: Jesus and His Modern Critics*. Louisville: Westminster John Knox, 2004.
———. "Parable and Kingdom. A Survey of the Evidence in Mark." *PRSt* 27 (2000) 179–99.
———. *Parables as Poetic Fictions: The Creative Voice of Jesus*. 1994. Reprinted, Eugene, OR: Wipf & Stock, 2005.
———. "Survivors of the Crucifixion: Searching for Profiles in the Parables." In *Hermeneutik der Gleichnisse Jesu: Methodische Neuensätze zum Verstehen urchristlicher Parabeltexte*, edited by Ruben Zimmerman and Gabi Kern, 165–80. WUNT 231. Tübingen: Mohr/Siebeck, 2008.
———. "The 34 Gospels: Diversity and Division among the Earliest Christians." *Bible Review* 18.3 (2002) 20–31, 46–47.
———. "Thomas and the Synoptics: Aiming at a Consensus." *SecCent* 7 (1989–1990) 39–56.
———. *When History and Faith Collide: Studying Jesus*. Peabody, MA: Hendrickson, 1999.
Higgins, A. J. B. "Non-Gnostic Sayings in the *Gospel of Thomas*." *NovT* 4 (1960) 292–306.
Hock, Ronald F. *The Infancy Gospels of James and Thomas with Introduction, Notes, and Original Text Featuring the New Scholars Version Translation*. The Scholars Bible 2. Santa Rosa, CA: Polebridge, 1995.
Immerwahr, Henry R. "New Wine in Ancient Wineskins: The Evidence from Attic Vases." *Hesperia* 61 (1992) 121–32.
Janssens, Yvonne. "The Trimorphic Protennoia and the Fourth Gospel." In *The New Testament and Gnosis: Essays in Honour of Robert McL. Wilson*, edited by A. H. B. Logan and A. J. M. Wedderburn, 229–44. Edinburgh: T. & T. Clark, 1983.
Jeremias, Joachim. *The Parables of Jesus*. Translated by S. H. Hooke. Rev. ed. New York: Scribner, 1963.

Bibliography

Johnson, Steven R. *Seeking the Imperishable Kingdom: Wealth, Wisdom, and a Jesus Saying.* Eugene, OR: Cascade Books, 2008.

King, Karen L. *The Gospel of Mary of Magdala: Jesus and the First Woman Apostle.* Santa Rosa, CA: Polebridge, 2003.

Kittel, Gerhard, and Gerhard Friedrich. *Theological Dictionary of the New Testament.* Translated by Geoffrey W. Bromiley. 10 vols. Grand Rapids: Eerdmans, 1964–1976.

Kloppenborg, John S. *The Tenants in the Vineyard: Ideology, Economics, and Agrarian Conflict in Jewish Palestine.* WUNT 195. Tübingen: Mohr/Siebeck, 2006.

Koester, Helmut. *Ancient Christian Gospels: Their History and Development.* Philadelphia: Trinity, 1990.

———. *Introduction to the New Testament.* Vol. 1, *History, Culture, and Religion of the Hellenistic Age.* 2nd ed. New York: de Gruyter, 1995.

———. *Introduction to the New Testament.* Vol. 2, *History and Literature of Early Christianity.* 2nd ed. New York: de Gruyter, 1995.

Layton, Bentley. *The Gnostic Scriptures: A New Translation with Annotations and Introductions.* Garden City, NY: Doubleday, 1987.

———, editor. *Nag Hammadi Codex II, 2–7 Together with XIII 2*, Brit. Lib. OR. 4926 (1), and P. Oxy. 1, 654, 655.* 2 vols. The Coptic Gnostic Library. NHS 20. Oxford: Clarendon, 1983.

Lewis, Naphtali. *Life in Egypt under Roman Rule.* Oxford: Clarendon, 1983.

Lips, Hermann von. "Schweine Füttert Man, Hund Nicht." *Zeitschrift für die neutestamentliche Wissenschaft* 79 (1988) 165–86.

Luibheid, Colm, translator. *Pseudo-Dionysius: The Complete Works.* Classics of Western Spirituality. New York: Paulist, 1987.

McGovern, Patrick E., et al., editors. *The Origins and Ancient History of Wine.* Luxembourg: Gordon & Breach, 1995.

Marxsen, Willi. *Introduction to the New Testament: An Approach to Its Problems.* Translated by G. Buswell. Philadelphia: Fortress, 1968.

Meier, John P. *A Marginal Jew: Rethinking the Historical Jesus.* 4 vols. Anchor Bible Reference Library. New York: Doubleday, 1991, 1994, 2001, 2009.

Meyer, Marvin, et al., editors. *Ancient Christian Magic: Coptic Texts of Ritual Power.* San Francisco: Harper SanFrancisco, 1994.

Meyer, Marvin. *The Gospel of Thomas: The Hidden Sayings of Jesus.* San Francisco: HarperSanFrancisco, 1992.

Miller, Robert J. *The Complete Gospels: Annotated Scholars Version.* Rev. and expanded ed. Sonoma, CA: Polebridge, 1994.

Mirecki, Paul Allen. "Manichaeans and Manichaeism." In *ABD* 4:502–11.

Nahm, Milton C., editor. *Selections from Early Greek Philosophy.* 3rd ed. New York: Appleton-Century-Crofts, 1947.

Parrott, Douglas M., editor. *Nag Hammadi Codices, III,3–4 and V,1 with Papyrus Berolinensis 8502,3 and Oxyrhynchus Papyrus 1081: Eugnostos and the Sophia of Jesus Christ.* NHS 27. Leiden: Brill, 1991.

Patterson, Stephen J., James M. Robinson, and Hans-Gephard Bethge. *The Fifth Gospel: The Gospel of Thomas Comes of Age.* Harrisburg, PA: Trinity, 1998.

Pearson, Birger A. "Alexandria." In *ABD* 1:152–57.

———. *Ancient Gnosticism: Traditions and Literature.* Minneapolis: Fortress, 2007.

Bibliography

Perrin, Norman. *The Kingdom of God in the Teaching of Jesus*. New Testament Library. Philadelphia: Westminster, 1963.

———. *The New Testament: An Introduction*. New York: Harcourt Brace Jovanovich, 1974.

Perry, B. E. *Babrius and Phaedrus: Newly Edited and Translated into English, Together with an Historical Introduction and a Comprehensive Survey of Greek and Latin Fables in the Aesopic Tradition*. LCL. Cambridge: Harvard University Press, 1984.

Plisch, Uwe-Karsten. *The Gospel of Thomas: Original Text with Commentary*. Translated by Gesine Schenke Robinson. Stuttgart: Deutsche Bibelgesellschaft, 2008.

Plotinus. *The Enneads*. Translated by Stephen MacKenna. London: Penguin, 1991.

Rad, Gerhard von, Walter Grundmann, and Gerhard Kittel. "Ἄγγελος." In *TDNT* 1:74–87.

Robinson, James M., editor. *The Facsimile Edition of the Nag Hammadi Codices. Cartonnage*. Leiden: Brill, 1979.

———. "Foreword." In *Nag Hammadi Codices: Greek and Coptic Papyri from the Cartonnage of the Covers*, edited by J. W. B. Barnes, et al., vii–x. NHS 16. Leiden: Brill, 1981.

———, general editor. *The Nag Hammadi Library in English*. 4th rev. ed. Leiden: Brill, 1996.

Robinson, James M., and Helmut Koester. *Trajectories through Early Christianity*. 1971. Reprinted, Eugene, OR: Wipf & Stock, 2006.

Rudolph, Kurt. *Gnosis: The Nature and History of Gnosticism*. Translated by Robert McLachlan Wilson. San Francisco: Harper & Row, 1983.

Schmidt, Carl, editor. *Pistis Sophia*. Translation and notes by Violet MacDermot. The Coptic Gnostic Library. NHS 9. Leiden: Brill, 1978.

———. *The Books of Jeu and the Untitled Text in the Bruce Codex*. Translation and notes by Violet MacDermot. The Coptic Gnostic Library. NHS 13. Leiden: Brill, 1978.

Schneemelcher, Wilhelm, and R. McL. Wilson, editors. *New Testament Apocrypha*. 2 vols. Rev. ed. Louisville: Westminster John Knox, 1991.

Schweizer, Eduard. "Σῶμα, σωματικός, σύσσωμος." In *TDNT* 7:1024–94.

Scott, Bernard Brandon. *Hear Then the Parable: A Commentary on the Parables of Jesus*. Minneapolis: Fortress, 1989.

Smallwood, E. Mary. *The Jews under Roman Rule: From Pompey to Diocletian; A Study in Political Relations*. Studies in Judaism in Late Antiquity 20. Leiden: Brill, 1976.

Stone, Michael E., and John Strugnell. *The Books of Elijah, Parts 1 and 2*. SBLTT 18. Pseudepigrapha 8. Missoula, MT: Scholars, 1979.

Strack, Hermann L., and Paul Billerbeck. *Kommentar zum Neuen Testament aus Talmud und Midrasch*. 4 vols. 5th ed. Munich: Beck, 1969.

Stroker, William D. *Extracanonical Sayings of Jesus*. Edited by Bernard Brandon Scott. SBL Resources for Biblical Study 18. Atlanta: Scholars, 1989.

Valantasis, Richard. *The Gospel of Thomas*. New Testament Readings. London: Routledge, 1997.

Wilson, R. McL. *Gnosis and the New Testament*. Philadelphia: Fortress, 1968.

Glossary

Modern sources used to develop the glossary are included in the bibliography.

Anchorite. Monasticism is known in two forms in the Christian West: anchorite monasticism and cenobite monasticism. Anchorites are monks who have withdrawn from normal society to lead solitary, ascetic, and celibate lives devoted to meditation, reflection, and prayer. Cenobites are monks who have withdrawn from normal society to lead lives of meditation, reflection, and prayer in communities of monks under a particular rule of faith. St. Anthony is believed to be the founder of anchorite monasticism and St. Pachomius is thought to be the founder of cenobite monasticism, both in the third and fourth centuries.

Aphorism. An aphorism is a terse, pithy sentence presenting an arresting precept or principle whose meaning is frequently unclear on the surface.

Clement. A Christian scholar, author, and teacher of the first Christian school, which was located in Alexandria in the second century. The school was designed to instruct converts in the truths of Christian faith. Clement was well read in the Hebrew Bible and early Christian writings and had an extensive knowledge of classical literature and philosophy.

Coptic. Coptic is the native language of Egypt evolving out of the ancient Egyptian hieroglyphs and receiving a standardized form around the beginning of the third century CE. It developed several dialects, and survives today, in the Bohairic dialect, as the liturgical language of the Coptic Christian Church.

Epiphanius. A fourth-century abbot of a Christian monastery, which he founded himself in Judea. Later he was elected bishop of Salamis on the

Glossary

island of Cyprus. An ardent opponent of heresy, he published a valuable work dedicated to describing and refuting the "heretics," i.e., the "Medicine Chest" written to serve as an antidote to the venom of the poisonous snakes—the heretics.

Eusebius. A fourth-century church leader and bishop of Caesarea. He is best known for his *Ecclesiastical History*, which brings him the status of the greatest historian of Christian antiquity.

Gnostic. The term is derived from a Greek word *gnosis*, which means knowledge. A Gnostic was one who claimed to posses a special intuited knowledge of the divine.

Gnosticism. The term Gnosticism is applied to rather widespread and diverse groups reflecting different but related religio-philosophical systems; it is documented by texts from the second century CE. In general these groups share an anti-cosmic and world-rejecting stance. They are dualistic in the sense that there is an irreparable breach between ultimate divine reality and the created order of things that can only be overcome by illumination from the divine world. These phenomena are primarily known in texts reflecting an awareness of Christianity, but there are also non-Christian texts that reflect Gnostic features. Scholars debate whether Gnosticism existed in the first century, since all extant texts are from the second century and later. Others argue that if the logic "no texts, no history" is applied, then Christianity itself is a second-century phenomenon, since no physical manuscripts from the early Christian movement exist in the first century.

Hellenistic. A term applied to the hybrid culture that emerged in the Mediterranean basin from the time of Alexander the Great (323 BCE) to the disintegration of the Roman Empire (ca. 410 CE). Alexander had intended to bring classical Greek culture to the peoples he conquered, but Greek culture blended with indigenous cultures to produce Hellenistic culture.

Hermetism. A system of ideas based on the eclectic teachings of Hermes Trismegistos (Thrice-great Hermes), a name for the Egyptian God Thot or Tat. Hermetic literature, likely originating in Egypt, in part, is occult—astrology, magic, and alchemy. The religio-philosophical texts are known as the *Corpus Hermeticum*, a collection dating from the second to the fifth centuries CE. The teaching usually takes the form of a dialogue between a revealer figure (Hermes) and a receiver of knowledge (Tat or Asclepius,). The teaching reveals mysteries about God (the One or Monad), the universe, and human salvation by means of special knowledge and ecstatic experience.

Historical Jesus. The term "Historical Jesus" describes what can be known of the Jewish man, Jesus of Nazareth, by evaluating early Christian texts on the basis of secular historical criticism.

Hippolytus. A Presbyter in the third-century church in Rome who was an author, opponent of heresy, and a critic of church practices. He wrote numerous commentaries on the Bible, most of which do not survive. He is best known for his ten books on the *Refutation of All Heresies*.

Imperial Rule. This term translates the Greek word *basileia*, which is traditionally translated "kingdom." In order to emphasize that the Greek word describes a sphere of influence rather than a location; imperial rule or reign is a better translation.

Irenaeus. A second-century theologian, author, and bishop of Lyons (Roman *Lugdunum* in Gaul). Irenaeus was a participant in the major controversies of the church in his day (for example, the threat of Gnosticism). His most important work was the *Unmasking and Refutation of the False Gnosis*.

Lacuna. A word used in the study of ancient texts to indicate that part of the text is missing because of a gap or hole.

Mani, Manichaeism. Manichaeism was one of the four great universal missionary religions of the ancient world along with Judaism, Christianity, and Islam. Mani was born in Iran in the third century CE and early in life was associated with a baptismal sect. After a vision he left the sect. Later he had another vision in which it was revealed to him that he was the Apostle of Light and the Seal of the Prophets (by whom he meant Buddha, Jesus, and Zoroaster). These religions were limited but he,

Glossary

Mani, was called to establish the true religion. Mani taught that originally two eternal principles existed: Good and evil or light and darkness. These had become mingled in the ancient past. At the end of the future time light will be separated from darkness and the Elect, who followed a path of extreme asceticism, will be gathered into the Kingdom of Light. The dark forces will be sealed in a bottomless pit. In the fourth-century Manichaeism was a serious competitor to Christianity.

Marcion. A second-century Christian and church reformer from Asia Minor. Nothing remains of his writings except quotations, summaries, and refutations by his opponents. He was excommunicated for his views, but spent time organizing churches over the Mediterranean basin from Carthage in the west to Syria in the east. He rejected the view of God represented in the Hebrew Bible, which Christians referred to as the Old Testament, which he rejected as Scripture. He also rejected the allegorical method of interpreting Scripture employed by Christianity in general. His canon of Scripture consisted of an abbreviated version of Luke and the Pauline letters: Romans through 2 Thessalonians plus Philemon. He either did not know the Pastoral Letters or rejected them as Scripture. He was the first to form a collection of Christian writings and to regard them as Scripture. The Marcionite churches spread into the same areas that catholic Christianity spread and survived in the east into the tenth century.

Messiah. The word is a transliteration of a Hebrew word meaning "the anointed." It is applied to the kings of Israel and Judah in the Hebrew Bible (once to the Persian King Cyrus, Isa 45:1). In late Jewish texts the term is applied to the eschatological king of the last days. Early Christians applied the term "anointed" (in Greek, *Christos*) to Jesus of Nazareth.

Monachos. A transliteration of a Greek word meaning single or solitary, and as a substantive it is translated monk.

Mystagogue. A teacher of sacred mysteries and ceremonies.

Mysticism. The experience of an immediate union or communion with ultimate divine reality through contemplation or meditation.

Glossary

Naasanes. The Naasenes are a radical "Christian" group of the second/third century described only by Hippolytus. Their name (likely chosen by Hippolytus himself) is derived from the Hebrew word for snake, which transliterated into Greek appears as *naas*. They, however, call themselves Gnostics, since they alone know the "deep things" (Rev 2:24). Hippolytus gives a summary of their teaching. They publicly venerate the snake met in the story of creation (Gen 3:1–19) and interpret the creation narrative allegorically. The first principle of the universe is Adamas, who is Man and also the Son of Man. Knowing Adamas produces the capacity for one to know God. Adamas is comprised of three principles: the intellectual, natural, and the material (Gen 2:7). These three elements come to reside in Jesus and through him have passed into the universe. Hence there are three ways of existing: angelic, natural, and earthly, and correspondingly those who exist in this way are characterized as the chosen, the called, and the captive.

Nag Hammadi Library. A collection of twelve books (codices not scrolls) and a few leaves of another individual writing (52 texts and parts of texts in all). The books were buried for safe keeping around the middle of the fourth century in Upper Egypt near the modern city of Nag Hammadi, hence the name of the collection, and discovered in 1945. The treatises were religio-philosophical in content, many of which were declared by Christian orthodoxy to be heretical in outlook.

Neo-Platonism. A modern term describing the attempt of Plotinus (third century CE) to renew Platonist philosophy. It was the most influential philosophical system from the third to the sixth centuries CE, that is, during the formative years of Christianity. Plotinus' writings were published by his student Porphyry from lectures Plotinus prepared for his students and arranged by Porphyry in six groups of nine each (The *Enneads*). Plotinus believed that everything emanated from the One, which is transcendent and the ground of all reality. Between the One and physical matter lay in a descending order three levels of consciousness: the Mind, the Soul, and Nature. Human beings possess the capability of all three levels of consciousness but beyond that there exists the possibility of unification with the One, which Plotinus is said to have achieved several times.

Glossary

Origen: He is usually described as the greatest Christian scholar and most prolific Christian writer of antiquity. As a youth he was appointed head of an ecclesiastical school in Alexandria and later ordained Priest in Caesarea. His allegorical interpretation of the Bible and the heavy influence of Platonic philosophy on him led him into intense controversy with others in the church. One of his most severe critics was Epiphanius of Salamis. Only a small number of his writings have been preserved.

Oxyrhynchus: The name of an ancient Egyptian city where British archaeologists 1896-1906 discovered massive amounts of ancient papyri in the city dump of the old city. The British Oxyrhynchus Papyri project has been publishing the finds since 1898 at the rate of about one volume a year, and today it is estimated that appromimately 100,000 unpublished papyri are stored in the Sackler Library in Oxford. This collection is the primary supplier of New Testament manuscripts to the scholarly world.

Parable: A parable in its classical form in the New Testament is a brief narrative relating a story (that is, a parable has plot, characters, and action) that begins and concludes, although the complication in the story is left unresolved. Scholars disagree on how the story functioned for Jesus. Today there are several scholarly theories for how the stories functioned in the time of Jesus.

Parallelism: Parallelism is a characteristic of Hebrew poetry, which balances ideas and concepts of one line to a second line. The second line can express the same thought of the first with different words (synonymous parallelism), express a contrasting idea to the thought in the first line (antithetical parallelism), or continue the thought of the first line into the second (synthetic parallelism).

Philo. Also Philo Judaeus. A first-century philosopher, writer, and political leader. Along with the first-century Jewish general, political leader, and writer Josephus, he was the most significant figure in the Jewish-Greek literary tradition. The greater part of his literary activity consisted of commentaries on the first five books of the Hebrew Bible. He draws on various schools of Greek philosophy in order to provide an allegorical interpretation of the Greek version (the Septuagint) of the Hebrew Bible.

Plato: A Greek philosopher of fifth/fourth century BCE Athens. He wrote dialogues featuring his teacher Socrates in discussions with interlocutors. The subject matter of the discussions concerned ethics and political thought, knowledge and its objects, the soul and the cosmos. Plato's theory of ideas, making a distinction between the eternal world of ideas (or forms) and the physical (or sensible) world of change, became a matrix for the development of thinking about philosophy and religion in the Greco-Roman period. Ideas are real in the sense that they have eternal existence outside the cosmic order. What exists in the world is only an imperfect imitation.

Plotinus. See Neoplatonism

Proverb. A proverb is a short pithy saying that strikingly summarizes some aspect of traditional wisdom. The proverb states what is instantly clear and recognized as true, right, and proper.

Q. In New Testament studies the letter Q (the first letter of a German word *Quelle*, meaning source) designates a hypothetical source used by Matthew and Luke in addition to their use of Mark as sources for the information in their gospels. It is hypothetical in the sense that no ancient manuscripts of Q have survived, although Q scholars argue that Q does survive in the agreements of Matthew and Luke against Mark.

Synoptic Gospels. Matthew, Mark, and Luke are called the Synoptic Gospels because they take a highly similar view of the public career of Jesus of Nazareth.

One. That is, singularity, unity, monad. A religio-philosophical concept and characteristic of the ground of all being, occurring in ancient Greek philosophy and religion. In philosophy the essential eternal unity of the ground of all Being is contrasted with the mutability and instability of the manifoldness of Matter.

Glossary

Septuagint. An ancient Greek translation of the Hebrew Bible containing some books not found in the Hebrew. The Torah (the first five books of the Hebrew Bible) was translated into Greek as early as the third century BCE. The Greek Septuagint rather than the Hebrew was used by the writers of the New Testament.

Valentinus. A Christian-Gnostic teacher and churchman of the second century CE, originally from Alexandria, Egypt, but he migrated to Rome. He founded a school of thought, called Valentinianism, which survived into the seventh century. He and his school were later regarded as heretics. An original thinker, some of his writings still survive, notably, the Nag Hammadi writing: *The Gospel of Truth.*

Index of Modern Authors

Allberry, C. R. C., 30, 137, 189
Allen, R. E., 102, 189
Altaner, B., 189
Attridge, H. W., 2, 3, 71, 189

Barnes, J. W. B., xi, 3, 193,
Bauer, W., 4, 5, 12, 189
Bell, H. I., 5, 189
Bethge, H.-G., 85, 191, 192
Betz, H. D., 189
Bierma, L. D., 191
Billerbeck, P., 86, 193
Broek, R. van den, 191
Bromiley, G. W., 192
Brown, R. E., 4, 189
Brown, S. G., 159, 189
Bultmann, R., 69, 86, 189
Buswell, G., 192

Charlesworth, J. A., 52, 189
Connolly, R. H., 99, 189
Copenhaver, B. P., 69, 88, 189
Crossan, J. D., 26, 181, 159

Dalman, G., 86, 189
Davies, S., 150, 166, 167, 190
DeConick, A. D., 22, 30, 71, 81, 82, 85, 86, 87, 93, 108, 128, 130, 156, 161, 169, 182, 190
Dillon, J. M., 190
Dodd, C. H., 16, 17, 190
Dodds, E. R., 190
Drijvers, H. J. W., 3, 190

Eliade, M., 190

Falconer, W. A., 158, 190
Ferguson, E., 51, 190
Freedman, D. N., 190
Friedrich, G., 192
Foerster, W., 55, 187, 190
Funk, R. W., 8, 15, 17, 75, 161, 190

Gardner, I., 27, 190
Gärtner, B., 16, 159, 179, 190
Ginzberg, L., 90, 190
Goodspeed, E. J., 190
Goodwin, W. W., 183, 190
Grant, R. M., 144, 162, 190
Grenfell, B. P., 2, 190, 191
Grobel, K., 189
Grundmann, W., 193
Guillaumont, A., ix, 4, 6, 191

Harnack, A. von, 191
Hanson, K. C., 50, 171, 191
Harkness, G., 10, 191
Hedrick, C. W., 8, 10, 15, 17, 32, 54, 84, 111, 120, 133, 147, 155, 167, 170, 180, 181, 191
Higgins, A. J. B., 17, 191
Hock, R. F., 2, 191
Holmén, T., 191
Hooke, S. H., 191
Hoover, R. W., 190
Hornblower, S., 190
Hunt, A. S., 2, 190, 191

Immerwahr, H. R., 97, 191

203

Index of Modern Authors

Janssens, Y., 16, 191
Jeremias, J., 125, 165, 191
Johnson, S., 139

Kern, G., 191
King, K. L., 31, 192
Kittel, G., 192, 193
Kloppenborg, J. S., 124, 125, 192
Koester, H., 3, 4, 12, 13, 16, 184, 192, 193
Kraft, B., 189
Krodel, G., 189

Lake, K., 190
Layton, B., 19, 20, 21, 22, 29, 26, 27, 28,
    30, 63, 65, 66, 68, 70, 71, 72, 73,
    74, 79, 80, 82, 83, 141, 182, 189,
    192
Levertoff, P. P., 189
Lewis, N., 5, 192
Lips, H. von, 161, 192
Logan, A. H. B., 191
Lubheid, C., 102, 192

MacDermot, V., 52, 56, 183, 193
McGovern, P. E., 97, 192
MacKenna, S., 193
Marsh, J., 189
Marxsen, W., 4, 192
Meier, J. P., 15, 192
Meyer, M., 127, 144, 186, 192
Miller, R. J., 64, 66, 168, 170, 174, 192
Mirecki, P., 192

Nahm, M., 48, 192

Parrott, D. M., 4, 192
Patterson, S. J., 85, 192
Pearson, B. A., 5, 192
Perrin, N., 4, 185, 192, 193
Perry, B. E., 31, 171, 193
Plisch, U.-K., 4, 105, 108, 124, 132, 136,
    147, 150, 154, 161, 164, 170, 183,
    193
Porter, S. E., 191

Quispel, G., 191

Rad, G. von, 154, 193
Robinson, G. S., 193
Robinson, J. M., ix, xi, 3, 85, 192, 193
Rudolph, K., 69, 193

Schenke, H.-M., 191
Schmidt, C., 193
Schoedel, W. R., 144, 162, 190
Schneemelcher, W., 2, 81, 87, 190, 193
Schweizer, E., 153, 193
Scott, B. B., 165, 193
Sharpe, E. J., 190
Smallwood, E. M., 5, 193
Smith, M., 189
Steely, J. E., 191
Spawforth, A., 190
Stone, M. E., 47, 193
Stroker, W. D., 25, 60, 62, 66, 77, 82, 171,
    181, 193
Strack, H. L., 86, 193
Strugnell, J., 47, 193
Szold, H., 190

Trask, W. R., 190

Valantasis, R., 86, 183
Vermaseren, M. J., 191, 193

Wedderburn, A. J. M., 191
Wilson, R. McL., 2, 16, 81, 87, 190, 191,
    193

Zimmerman, R., 191

Index of Ancient Sources

OLD TESTAMENT/ HEBREW BIBLE/SEPTUAGINT

Genesis
1:26–31	151
1:26–30	183
1:26–27	151
1:28	144
1:31	183
2:7	69, 100, 173, 184, 186, 199
2:2–3	66
2:4–22	36
2:4–7	151
2:8–10	52
2:9	52
2:16	52
2:18–23	36, 173
2:21–23	60, 186
2:24	137
2:25	81
3:1–22	90
3:1–19	199
3:5	90
3:7	81
3:10	81
3:22	52, 90
4:1	90
15:6	10
17:1–14	106
19:24	33, 147
22:1–14	10

Exodus
3:2–4	33
3:2	147
4:15	179
9:23–24	147
12:48	106
13:21–22	33, 147
16:25–30	66
19:18	147
21:4	133
23:12	66
22:25	163
24:16–17	148
33:17–23	148
33:20–23	113
34:21	66

Leviticus
12:3	106
13:52	147
19:18	64
19:33–34	64
24:16	40
25:35–37	163

Numbers
31:23	147

Deuteronomy
4:23–24	33
4:24	147
6:4	177

Index of Ancient Sources

Deuteronomy (*continued*)

9:3	147
10:16	106
15:3–4	64
15:11	17
20:5–8	121
23:19–20	163
24:5	121
25:5–10	55
30:6	106
32:30	62

Judges

6:17	40
6:21	40
14:10–18	133

Ruth

4:7–9	55

1 Samuel

18:7	62

Job

1:21	68
4:8–9	135
8:22	80
14:1–5	44
15:14	44
25:4–6	152
25:4	44
32:18–19	97
42:5–6	113

Psalms

1:1–3	52
8:3–6	152
12:2	177
18:2	52
18:6–9	147
31:3	52
35:26	80
37:30	179
39:4	48
42:2	13, 81
42:9	52
49:3	179
71:3	52
78:2	47
82:7	71
84:2	13, 81
89:45	80
91:7	62
118:22	126
126:5–6	135
132:18	80
143:4	87

Proverbs

1:28	82
5:15	136
8:58	179
10:11	136
10:31	179
17:2	133
30:13	94

Ecclesiastes

1:6	49
1:9	49
3:7	134
7:28	62
12:7	49

Isaiah

5:1–7	85
5:15	94
6:1	113
6:5	113
7:14	105
10:16–17	147
11:1–5	25
30:14	136
33:10–14	147

34:4	183	Joel	
37:4	13, 81	3:13	58
37:17	13, 81		
38:11	113	Amos	
44:6	49	5:11–15	90
46:10	49		
60:21	85	Micah	
61:1	107	1:11	80
64:4	47	3:1–4	90
		6:6–8	28
Jeremiah		6:7	62
1:50	50	7:6	45, 46
2:13	136		
4:4	106	Zechariah	
5:14	33	2:5	33, 147
10:10	13	14:6–8	52
12:13	133	14:9	177
13:26	80, 81		
14:3–4	136	Malachi	
14:3	136	2:10	177
20:9	33	2:15	177
23:28–32	147		
23:29	33		
32–39	177		

Ezekiel

1:26–28	148
3:8–9	52
11:19	177
17:22–23	54

APOCRYPHA/SEPTUAGINT

2 Esdras

6:1–6	49
6:55–59	37
7:10–11	37
9:1–6	49
12:3–39	19
14:1–5	19
14:45	105

Daniel

2:22	19
2:30	19
4:20–21	54
6:26	81
7:13–14	152

Judith

9:2	80

Hosea

2:4–5	175
6:6	28
10:10	135

Index of Ancient Sources

Wisdom of Solomon

8:19–20	100

Sirach

4:7	167
6:19	32
8:1–3	167
9:10	96
11:18–19	120
20:1–7	134
24:21	179
26:29–27:2	122
27:6	93
31:28	96
32:6	96
48:1	33
51:26–27	157

1 Maccabees

1:28	80
1:59–61	144

2 Maccabees

8:4	81

PSEUDEPIGRAPHA

Apocalypse of Moses

37:4–6	151
39:1–3	151

3 Baruch

4:7–17	52

Book of Baruch (Latin)

	82

1 Enoch

8:1–8	52
37–71	19

4 Ezra

7:25	86
8:52	52

Testament of Moses

11:16	105

NEW TESTAMENT

Matthew

1:18–21	44
1:20–23	105
3:9	51
3:10	85
3:11–12	33
3:12	58
4:3	51
4:17	28
5:3–12	112
5:3	28, 107
5:6	67, 130
5:8	66, 113, 129
5:10	128
5:11–12	112
5:11	128
5:14	73, 102
5:15	73, 75
5:18	34
5:23–34	163
5:25	129
5:31–32	7
5:42	163
5:43–44	64
5:44	163

Index of Ancient Sources

Reference	Page	Reference	Page
5:48	127	11:7–10	94
6:1	41	11:7–8	142
6:3	119	11:10	154
6:2–4	41	11:11	44, 94
6:5–6	41	11:12–14	94
6:11	79	11:15	31
6:13–20	38	12:22–30	77
6:16–18	41	11:28–30	112, 157
6:20	139	11:28	157
6:21	93	11:29	157
6:22–23	63, 177	12:29	77, 102
6:24	95	11:30	157
6:25–34	79	12:31–32	91
6:33	139	12:33	90
7:2	9	12:34	93
7:3–5	65	12:35	43, 93
7:6	161	12:36–37	93
7:7–11	159	12:38–39	7
7:7	162	12:47–50	168
7:14	112	12:49	168
7:15	92	13:3–8	32
7:16–20	90	13:9	31
7:16–17	111	13:10–17	xi
7:16	92	13:11	19, 118
8:20	152	13:12	86
8:22	34, 157	13:16–17	47
9:9	4, 87	13:17	82
9:14–15	173	13:18–23	32, 110
9:16	98	13:19–23	32
9:37–38	135	13:24–30	110
9:67	97	13:24	110
10:1	42	13:27	110
10:3	4	13:29–30	110
10:8	42	13:31–32	54
10:16	84, 169, 170	13:31	28
10:26	23, 27	13:33	165
10:27	74	13:35	82
10:28	184	13:36–43	110
10:34–36	46	13:37–43	135
10:35	45, 47	13:43	31
10:37–38	108	13:44	138, 180, 167
10:37	170	13:45–46	138, 167
11:7–11	142	13:47–48	31

Index of Ancient Sources

Matthew (*continued*)

Reference	Page
13:49–50	110
13:51–52	58
13:57	72
15:10–16	9
15:11	9, 43
15:12–14	9
15:14	9, 76
15:15–20	9
15:17–20	43
15:18–20	93
15:18	129
16:1–8	28
16:1–4	7
16:1	158
16:2–3	27, 158
16:3	158
16:13–20	39
16:16–19	39
16:16–18	28
16:19	83
16:24	108
17:1–8	80
17:20	51, 99
18:1–5	25
18:2–4	55
18:6	xi
18:7	122
18:8–9	112
18:10	xi, 178
18:12–13	xi, 177
18:14	xi, 178
18:19	99
19:4–6	60
19:9	7
19:12	169
19:13–15	55
19:17	112
19:21	119, 127, 163
19:27	119
19:30	26
20:16	26
20:25	142
21:19	51
21:21–22	99
21:22	51
21:33–41	124
21:42	126
21:43	126
21:45	126
22:1–14	121
22:14	62
22:39	64, 163
23:2–3	83
23:13–25	156
23:13–15	171
23:13	76, 83, 171
23:16	76
23:23	171
23:24	76
23:25	171
23:26	156
23:27	171
23:29	171
24:3	48
24:4	77
24:19–21	144
24:23	185
24:26–27	185
24:35	34
24:43	56
25:1–13	173
25:1–12	137
25:13	173
25:27	163
25:29	86
25:35–40	130
26:11	17
28:1	55
28:19–28	74
28:19	91

Mark

Reference	Page
1:6	142
1:8	33
1:14	28, 87

Index of Ancient Sources

1:15	14	7:20–22	129
1:17	157	7:18–23	43
2:14	157	8:14–21	59
2:18–20	173	8:15	165
2:18–22	41	8:27–29	39
2:21	98	8:31	37
2:22	97	8:34–37	153
3:22–27	77, 152	8:34	108
3:22	51	8:38	152
3:27	77, 172	9:1	14
3:28–29	91	9:2–8	80
3:31–35	168	9:30–32	37
4:2	13	9:35	163
4:3–8	32	9:42–48	108
4:9	31	9:43–47	41
4:10–25	xi, 8	9:43	112
4:10–12	8, 159	9:45	112
4:10	8	9:47	14, 60, 112
4:14–19	166	10:6–8	60, 137
4:11–12	47	10:13–15	55
4:11	8, 19, 118, 159	10:15	14, 60
4:13–20	8, 32, 110	10:21	119, 127, 153, 157, 163
4:14–20	32	10:25	169, 60
4:18–19	122	10:28	119
4:21–23	8	10:31	26
4:21	75	10:33–34	37
4:22	27	11:14	51
4:23	31	11:20–21	51
4:24	8	11:21–24	99
4:25	9, 86	11:24	51
4:29	58	12:1–9	124
4:30	28	12:10	126
4:31–32	54	12:12	126
5:29	153	12:13–17	169
6:4	72	12:29–30	177
6:21	167	12:31	64
6:35–44	51	12:34	14, 60
6:45–52	51	13	185
7:2–5	156	13:3–4	48
7:14–15	9	13:17–19	144
7:15	43	13:20	100
7:17–23	9	13:21	185
7:20–23	93	13:26	152

Index of Ancient Sources

Mark (continued)

Reference	Page
13:31	34
14:7	17
14:22	153
14:32–42	108
14:62	152
15:21	87
15:28	105
15:40	117
16:1	55, 117
16:15–16	74
16:17–18	51

Luke

Reference	Page
1:42	143
1:48	143
1:51	129
1:78–79	63
2:7	44
2:16	55
2:41–47	25
3:8	51
3:9	85
3:16–17	33
4:3	51
4:16–20	112
4:23	72
4:24	72
5:33–35	173
5:35	173
5:36	98
5:37–38	96, 97
5:39	96
6:20–23	112
6:20	28, 107, 169
6:21	130
6:22–23	112
6:22	128
6:24–26	153
6:26	128
6:27–28	64
6:27	163
6:30	163
6:34–35	163
6:37–38	9
6:39–40	76
6:39	9, 76
6:40	9
6:41–42	65
6:43–44	90, 111
6:43	92
6:45	43, 92, 93, 128, 142
7:24–28	94
7:24–27	94
7:24	142, 154
7:28	44, 94
8:2–3	55
8:5–8	32
8:8	31
8:9–24	xi
8:10	19, 118
8:11–15	32, 110
8:16	75
8:17	27
8:18	86
8:19–21	168
8:20–21	168
9:18–21	39
9:23–24	87
9:23	108
9:28–36	80
9:52	154
9:58	152
9:59	157
9:60	34
9:62	119, 139
10:2	135
10:8–9	42
10:21	82
10:22	24
10:23–24	47
10:24	82
10:27	64
11:9–13	15

Index of Ancient Sources

11:9	42, 162	14:35	31
11:13	79	15:1–3	xi, 178
11:14–23	77	15:4–6	xi, 167
11:21–22	77	15:4	177
11:26	26	15:5–6	177
11:27–28	143	15:7	xi, 178
11:28	112	16:1–7	167
11:33	75	16:8	102
11:34–35	63	16:13	95
11:34	177	16:16	94
11:37–44	156	16:17	34
11:40	156	17:6	99
11:42–43	171	17:16	51
11:52	83, 171	17:20–21	22, 185
12:2	23, 27, 29	17:22–37	116
12:3	74	17:22	82, 116
12:4	153	17:23–24	185
12:10	91	17:30–31	116
12:13–14	133	17:34–35	116
12:15–21	133	18:1–8	20
12:16–20	120	18:1	8
12:20	120	18:2–5	8, 133
12:21	146	18:6–8	8
12:22–31	79	18:14	26
12:22	6	18:15–17	55
12:31	139, 163	18:22	127, 119, 163
12:33	119, 139, 163	19:23	163
12:39	56	19:26	86
12:49	33	20:9–16	124
12:51–53	46	20:17	126
12:51	45	20:18	126
12:54–56	27, 158	20:20–26	169
12:56	58, 158	20:34–36	153
13:7	85	21:7	48
13:18	28	21:23–24	144
13:19	54	21:33	34
13:20–21	165	21:34	166
13:30	26	23:27–31	144
14:16–24	121	23:29	144
14:26–27	108	23:43	52
14:26	170	24:27	105
14:28–32	167		
14:33	119		

Index of Ancient Sources

John

1:1–4	140
1:1–3	50
1:1	47
1:4–8	102
1:4	112
1:5	63
1:10	57
1:12–13	94
1:14	37, 44, 50, 67, 80
1:16	127
1:18	44, 66, 113, 148
1:29	57
1:39	157
1:43	157
1:45	105
2:1–11	51
3:3–8	94
3:4	60
3:16–21	185
3:17–19	77
3:19–21	63
3:35	117
3:36	112, 185
4:6–7	24
4:10	158
4:13–14	179
4:14	136, 185
4:35–38	135
4:44	72
5:20	24
5:21	185, 185
5:24–25	185
5:24	20, 112
5:26	112
5:39	105
5:40	112
6:33	112, 185
6:35	112
6:39–40	77, 185
6:44	77
6:46	66, 113
6:48	112
6:51	35
6:53	112
6:54	185
6:57	19
6:63	33, 112
6:66–69	82
6:68	33
7:7	57
7:33–34	82
7:37–38	179
7:37	67
7:38	105
7:42	105
8:12	63, 102, 112, 140
8:21	82
8:31	51
8:39–41	175
8:51	20
8:58	50
9:5	102, 140
10:10	112
10:16	26, 177
10:25	112
10:30–33	40
10:30	26, 147, 177
10:34	71
11	3
11:1	55
11:24–26	185
11:25–26	20
12:5	164
12:8	17
12:24–25	87, 88
12:31	185
12:35–36	63
12:36	102, 67
12:40	67
12:46	63, 67, 140
12:48	185
12:49	117
13:17	143
13:29	164
13:33	82
14:1–7	183

14:3	37	20	3
14:6	112	20:8	150
14:7	24	20:22	82
14:8–11	26	20:29	112
14:9	66, 147	20:31	112
14:12	51	21:19	157
14:13–14	159	21:22	157
14:15–17	38		
14:16–19	82	Acts	
14:16–17	57	1:3	19
14:18–19	37, 91	1:8	74
14:19	82	2:3–4	33
14:25–26	38, 82, 91	2:10	5
14:25	37	2:42	174
15:5–6	85	2:44–45	79
15:5	80	3:6–8	51
15:7	51, 159	4:10	51
15:13	64	4:11	126
15:14	51	4:32	177
15:15	117	7:27–28	133
15:18–19	57	7:35	133
15:26	38, 91	8:1–5	5
16:3	24	8:37	101
16:4–5	159	9:36–41	51
16:5–7	37	10:1–34	42
16:7–13	38	10:30	174
16:12–13	159	10:40–41	19
16:16–19	37, 82	11:19–20	5
16:24	159	12:1–5	5
16:25–28	37	12:12–15	154
16:28	67	12:12	55
17:3	24	13:2–3	41, 174
17:11	26, 57	13:6–11	51
17:14–16	183	13:30–31	19
17:14	57	14:15	81
17:16	57	14:23	174
17:18	67	18:28	105
17:20–23	26, 177	19:11–12	51
17:21	177	20:7	66
17:24	80, 183	20:22–25	108
18:36	57	22:13–16	74
18:37	67	26:12–18	74
19:25	55	28:1–6	51

Index of Ancient Sources

Romans

Reference	Page
1:2	105
1:21–23	49
1:21	67
2:1	65
2:5	67
2:19	63
2:25–29	106
2:29	106
3:27–31	106
3:30	177
4:20	77
5:14	151
5:17	21
5:18	112
6:3–4	81
6:6–9	87, 88
6:12	69
8:2	112
8:6	112
8:9–11	23, 184
8:9	70
8:13	70
8:18–23	183
8:19	82
8:29–30	100
8:38–39	101
11:2	100
11:15	57
11:25–29	19
11:25	118
11:36	140
12:1	69
12:2	66
12:4–5	26
12:5	36, 177, 179
12:8	163
12:9–21	45
12:16	65
12:17	164
12:20–21	164
12:20	64
13:8–10	45
13:8	64
13:9–10	64
13:12	57
14	159
14:1–8	42
14:10	65
15:1–2	65
15:1	77
15:18–20	74
15:25–29	79
16:6	55
16:25–27	82, 118
16:25–26	75
16:26	105

1 Corinthians

Reference	Page
1:17–25	47
1:18–29	25
1:20	57
2:1–3:4	159
2:6–9	20
2:7–15	56
2:7	13, 47, 118
2:9	13, 47
2:12–16	447
2:14	100
2:15–3:1	100
3:1–4	159
3:1	13
3:8	177
3:19	57
4:3–4	149
4:8	13, 21, 146
4:10	77
5:5	184
5:6–8	165
6:15–16	60
6:16–17	26, 177
6:17	36, 179, 186
7:1–40	46, 144
7:5	57, 153, 174
7:7–8	153
7:17–31	185

Index of Ancient Sources

7:19	106
7:29–31	110
7:29	153
7:31–35	122
7:31	87
7:32–38	153
8	159
8:3	24
8:4–6	177
8:6	140
8:7–13	42
8:8	28
8:10–12	65
9:16	108
9:19–25	108
10:17	26, 177
10:25–30	42
11:1	157
11:7–12	186
11:19	76
12:8	58
12:10	27, 51, 58, 154
12:12–17	26
12:12–13	36, 177, 179
12:20	177
12:26	26
12:28–29	154
12:28	51
13:2	51, 99, 127
13:4–7	45
15:22	151
15:28	140
15:36–39	87, 88
15:42–50	55
15:42–45	87, 88
15:47–48	100
15:50	70
15:51	118
16:1–4	29
16:2	66
16:13	77

2 Corinthians

3:15–16	67
4:4	67
4:16	87, 88
5:1–4	55
5:9	57
5:17	80, 87, 88
6:10	146
6:14	63
6:16	81
8–9	77
8:9	146
8:23	154
9:5–7	163
9:6–12	135
12:1–2	34
12:4	52
13:5	23, 65

Galatians

1:4	122
1:6–9	76
1:18–24	74
2:1–13	106
2:10	77
2:11–21	76
2:11–14	42
2:15–16	10
2:20	23, 179
3:6–9	10
3:6	10
3:8	105
3:20	177
3:22	105
3:28–29	61
3:28	14, 26, 177
4:4	44
4:9	24
4:19	23
4:21–31	52
5:6	106
5:7–10	165
5:14	64

Index of Ancient Sources

Galations (continued)

5:17	184
5:26	65
6:1–3	65
6:1	65, 77
6:7–9	135
6:15	106

Ephesians

1:9–10	118
1:22–23	141
1:23	127
2:1	34
2:2	122
2:5	34
2:14–18	26
2:14–15	177
3:2–6	56
3:3–10	118
3:4–6	82
3:8–10	82
3:19	127
4:1–3	45
4:6	141
4:10	141
4:13	127
4:22–24	80, 87, 88
4:28	153
5:8	102
5:15–16	158
5:28–32	118
5:31–32	60
6:5	177
6:10–17	77
6:11–18	166
6:11–13	57
6:12	101
6:18–19	75
6:19	118

Philippians

1:27	177
2:3	65
2:5–11	67
2:5–8	80
2:9–11	80
2:16	112
2:25	154
3:3	106
4:11–12	79
4:15–18	79
4:19	79

Colossians

1:15–20	11, 140
1:15	113, 149
1:17	141
1:19	23, 127
1:24–28	75, 118
1:27	23
2:2	66, 118
2:9	23, 127
2:15	101
2:16	42
3:4	112
3:9–10	80, 87, 88
3:11	140
3:22	177
4:3	118
4:5–6	58
4:12	127

1 Thessalonians

1:6	157
1:8–9	74
1:9	81
3:5	57
5:2	172
5:5	102
5:14–15	65
5:23	184

2 Thessalonians

2:1–5	76

Index of Ancient Sources

1 Timothy
1:16	112
1:17	148
2:5	177
2:13–14	151
3:6	67
3:16	67, 118
5:9–16	79
5:18	105
6:7–8	79
6:15–16	113
6:16	102, 148

2 Timothy
1:8–9	100
1:15	76
2:1	77
2:12	21, 146
2:15	84
2:16–18	76
2:22–26	77
3:15	105
3:16	105
4:10	122, 166

Titus
3:10–11	76

Hebrews
1:3	141
1:12	183
2:8–9	80
3:12–14	166
3:12	129
3:16–4:10	66
4:12	184
9:26	67
10:1	149
10:5	67
11:5	150
11:27	113, 148
11:37–38	109
12:8	175
12:14	80, 113
12:29	147
13:8	50

James
1:8	177
1:12	112
1:17	102
1:21	184
1:25	143
1:27	57, 66, 79, 112, 122, 130
2:1–7	107
2:1–5	164
2:5	146
2:8–9	45
2:8	64
2:15–16	79
2:17	10
2:21–24	10
2:23	10, 105
2:25	154
3:11–12	92
3:13–18	58
4:4	122
4:8	129, 177
4:11	65
5:1–6	146
5:14–15	51
5:20	184

1 Peter
1:1–2	100
1:3–5	82
1:9	184
1:12	82
1:20	82
2:7	126
2:11	184
2:17	45
2:19	112
2:21	157
5:8–9	166
5:8	30

Index of Ancient Sources

2 Peter

1:4	122
1:10	100
1:16–19	80
1:20	105
2:1	76
2:20–22	166
2:20	122
3:10	172
3:16	105

1 John

1:1–4	37
1:5–7	63
1:5	102
2:8	87
2:10	64
2:15–16	122
2:15	6
2:16	15
2:17	87
2:29	94
3:2	80
3:10	64
4:2–3	37
4:7–11	45
4:7	94
4:12	148
4:20	113
4:21	64
5:19	122

2 John

5–10	154

3 John

7–12	154
11	66

Revelation

1:1–3	19
1:4	44
1:7	80
1:8	44, 48
1:9–18	80
1:18	13, 19
2:1	154
2:7	31, 52
2:8	154
2:9	146
2:11	31
2:12	154
2:18	154
2:24	199
2:29	31
3:1	154
3:3	172
3:6	31
3:7	154
3:9	31
3:13	31
3:14	154
3:17	153
3:18	80
3:22	31
4:3–5	148
4:14–20	135
6:15	142
6:14	183
14:4	157
14:15–16	58
16:14–15	172
16:15	167
17:2	67
20:4	20
20:6	21
20:11	113
21:1–4	183
21:6	44, 49, 140
21:23	102, 148
22:5	148
22:13	44, 49, 140

Index of Ancient Sources

DEAD SEA SCROLLS

Commentary on Habakkuk   20
Commentary on Isaiah   20

RABBINIC WRITINGS

Bekhorot
4:6   133

GRECO-ROMAN WRITINGS

Aesop
Fable 702   171

Apostolic Constitutions
7:40–41   102

Asclepius (Corp. herm.)
8–10   69

Aristotle
Metaphysics
x.3.3   117

Augustine
Contra adversarum legis et prophetarum
2.4.14   105

Cicero
De divination   158

Clement of Alexandria
Excerpts from Theodotus
21.3   186
52.1   77

Letter to Theodore
1:17–18   159
1:21–23   159
2:2   159

Paedagogus
3.1   23

Salvation of the Rich (Quis div.)
25   129

Stromata
2.9.45   21
4.6.41   128
5.14.96   21
6.15.124.5–6   75
7.82.6–7   84

Corpus hermeticum
1.15   69
1.18   69
1.17–18   60
1.21   100
1.24–26   88
1.27   67
5   113
7.2–3   69
10.15–18   69
10.25   88
12.1–4   69
14.1   159

Index of Ancient Sources

Cyprian of Carthage

Treatise XII: ad Quirinum

3.29	82

Cyril of Jerusalem

Catechetical Lectures

4.36	2
6.31	2

Catechetical Lectures (On the Mysteries)

20.2	81

Didascalia Apostolorum

15:25	99

Epiphanius

Refutation of All Heresies

2.23.1	100

Epistula Apostolorum

47	76

Eusebius

Ecclesiastical History

2.23	37
2.23.4–18	37
3.2	5
3.5	5
3.25.6	1

Heraclitus

Fragment 70	48

Hesiod

Works and Days

109–201	48

Hippolytus

Refutation of All Heresies

5.7.20	1, 25
5.7.25	102
5.7.35	126
5.8.32	35
5.8.44	55, 186
5.9.6	54
5.16.1	88

Irenaeus

Demonstration of the Apostolic Preaching

43	50

Against Heresies

1.7.1	55
1.21.5	101

Josephus

Jewish Antiquities

4.8.49	105

Jewish War

4.1.1–10	73

Justin Martyr

Dialogue with Trypho

19:3	106

First Apology

30	51
61	61
67	66

Lactantius

The Divine Institutes

4.8	50

Index of Ancient Sources

Nicephorus

Stichometry   2

Origen

Against Celsus

1.38	51
8.15.16	136

First Principles

1.6.2	47

Homilae in Jeremiam

20.3	1, 147

Homilae in Lucam

1	1

Pausanias

Description of Greece

10.24.1	23

Philo

Allegorical Interpretation

1.31–32	148

On the Life of Moses

2.3.135	105
2.35.187–88	105

On Planting

36–37	52

Plato

Parmenedes

162B–163B	102

Phaedo

74–76	117

Republic

6:17–19	148
6:20	148
7:1–2:5	148

Timaeus

9–13	69
51B–52C	150

Pliny

Natural History

14.4.21	96
14.4.31–32	96
18.21.94–95	32

Plotinus

Enneads

IV.8.1–11	44
V.1.10–12	44
VI.9.3	102
VI.9.8–11	23, 88

Plutarch

Moralia

17E	47

Porphyry

Vita Plotini

23	23

Pseudo-Clementines

Recognitions

2.60	78

Pseudo-Dionysius Areopagita

Celestial Hierarchy

4.180C	113

Divine Names

1.597B	113

Ecclesiastical Hierarchy

392C	24

Index of Ancient Sources

Pseudo-Dionysius Areopagita (cont.)

Ecclesiastical Hierarchy (cont.)

393A–397A	102
396B–D	81
404C	81
536B	81

Epistles

1.1065A/B	113
5.1073A	113

Sextus Empiricus

Against the Mathematicians

1.123	47

Simplicius

In Aristotelis Physica commentaria

5	48

Virgil

Eclogue

4, lines 4–5	48

~

APOSTOLIC FATHERS

Barnabas

6:2	126
6:4	126
8:7	76
9:4	76
19:5	64
19:9	64
21:8	184

1 Clement

49:6	184

2 Clement

5:4–5	184
9:1–4	184
9:11	168
12:2–5	61
12:2–4	184

Didache

1:1–6:3	101
1:5–6	164
2:7	64
4:8	79
7:1	101
8:1–3	174
8:1–2	76
8:1	41
11–13	42, 254
11:1–2	76
11:3–6	154
11:7–13:7	154
12:3–4	79
13:1–7	79
14	66

Diognetus

6:3	57

Ignatius

To Polycarp

2:2	84

Shepherd of Hermas

Similitudes

4.4.5–7	122
5.1.1–5	41
5.2.5–8	41
5:5.1–5	66

5.5.2	85
5.6.2	85
6.5	69
8.8.1	122

NEW TESTAMENT APOCRYPHA

Acts of John

76	87

Acts of Thomas

47	39

Acts of Peter

39	140

Gospel of the Ebionites

Fragment 5	168

Gospel of the Egyptians (Greek) 81

Gospel of the Hebrews

Fragment 2	174
Fragment 4a	170
Fragment 4b	170
Fragment 4c	170
Fragment 6a	21
Fragment 6b	21
Fragment 7	64

Gospel of Judas

35:6–36:9	39
35:7–25	80
47:1–58	39
52–53	69

Gospel of Mary

8:12–19	185
10:1–6	38
10:9–17:7	39

Gospel of Peter

9	66

Gospel of the Savior

99:3–18	108
107:1–30	80
107:43–48	147
5F: 19–32	107
5H: 53–63	108

Gospel of Thomas (Infancy) 1

Pistis Sophia

Book 1: chap. 3	183
Book 2: chap. 86	52
Book 2: chap. 95	157
Book 3: chap. 120	56
Book 3: chap. 121	56

Q[uelle]

15, 33, 46, 47, 51, 56, 65, 74, 76, 79, 83, 86, 91, 92, 93, 94, 95, 107, 108, 111, 116, 128, 135, 139, 142, 152, 156, 157, 158, 159, 165, 165, 177

Second Book of Jeu

Chap. 50	52

Index of Ancient Sources

NAG HAMMADI CODICES

Apocalypse of Adam
64:20–28	186

1 Apocalypse of James
32:28–34:20	101

2 Apocalypse of James
55:15–57:11	37

Apocalypse of Paul
18:3–23	25
23:1–24:8	101

Apocalypse of Peter
81:17–18	19
82:17–83:15	37
83:1–15	19
83:15–84:6	86

Apocryphon of James
6:19–20	170

Apocryphon of John
II,1,9:8–10	49
II,1,15:1–23:35	69

Authoritative Teaching
34:1–18	137

Dialogue of the Savior
120:26	100
124:3	87
129:13–14	146

Discourse on the Eighth and Ninth
62:19–20	87

Eugnostos
III,3,70:18–73:3	44
III,3,74:20–75:23	44
III,3,78:9–12	117

Exegesis on the Soul
132:6–133:6	137

Gospel of Philip
52:21–24	175
52:25–35	135
54:19	150
55:6–14	35
55:19–22	135
56:20–26	70
56:26–57:22	55
64:9–12	50
65:1–26	174
68:22–26	186
69:1–70:4	137
69:8–14	148
70:9–22	137, 173, 186
73:19–23	115
75:21–25	81
76:17–22	86
81:34–85:26	137
85:29–31	85

Gospel according to Thomas
P. Oxy. 1	2, 7, 71
P. Oxy. 654	2, 3, 7
P. Oxy. 655	2, 7
Prologue	11, 13, 19, 25, 113, 140, 147
1	ix, 7, 12, 17, 20, 33, 47, 53, 67, 74, 77, 91, 110, 118, 151, 162, 179, 180, 184
2	7, 13, 21, 33, 45, 46, 47, 74, 118, 119, 144, 146, 150, 157, 162, 180, 184
3	x, 7

Index of Ancient Sources

3A	7, 10, 12, 22, 54, 60, 126, 142, 156, 165, 185	14C	9, 42, 43, 93, 156
3B	10, 11, 12, 13, 17, 19, 22, 23, 25, 36, 38, 44, 49, 56, 63, 67, 70, 86, 88, 91, 102, 104, 105, 106, 107, 109, 126, 127, 129, 131, 142, 146, 152, 165, 179, 183, 186	15	11, 44, 50, 91, 94
		16	x, 57
		16A	x, 11, 33, 45, 46, 63, 67, 126, 133, 167
		16B	x, 6, 12, 26, 46, 62, 67, 100, 104, 108, 122, 126, 132, 137, 138, 146, 153, 168
4	x, 7, 31	17	6, 11, 13, 27, 29, 47, 63, 67, 118, 149, 159, 162, 179
4A	x, 25, 27, 32, 45, 50, 55, 56, 94, 112, 119, 167, 177	18	ix, 10, 11, 14, 48, 49, 53, 59, 62, 89, 100, 102, 110, 140, 179, 183
4B	x, 26, 31, 36, 46, 60, 62, 99, 102, 128, 153, 177, 179		
5	7, 13, 27, 29, 31, 32, 47, 73, 118, 149, 158, 162, 179	19	x, 102
		19A	11, 50, 100, 102, 107, 112, 128, 129, 130, 143, 144, 172
6	ix, x, 6, 7, 12, 13	19B	13, 42, 51, 99, 157
6A	12, 23, 28, 29, 41, 42, 45, 54, 59, 66, 89, 106, 107, 130, 142, 156, 157, 163, 173	19C	33, 52, 151
		20	ix, 22, 32, 33, 54, 55, 56, 66, 89, 107, 108, 110, 125, 165, 177
6B	7, 27, 28, 29, 32, 47, 66, 73, 74, 118, 149, 162, 179	21	ix, x, 6
7	7, 16, 30, 35, 112	21A	11, 32, 55, 56, 59, 81, 89, 94, 125, 165
8	ix, 6, 26, 31, 32, 54, 56, 58, 63, 68, 120, 122, 135, 136, 137, 138, 165, 167, 177	21B	55, 56, 57, 132, 166, 172
		21C	11, 34, 55, 57, 58, 66, 77, 109, 114, 120, 122, 142, 146, 153, 163, 172, 182
9	6, 31, 32, 54, 55, 56, 68, 77, 110, 120, 121, 125, 135, 138, 165, 177, 180	21D	55, 56, 58, 110, 135, 166
10	6, 8, 11, 33, 45, 46, 57, 63, 110, 147, 167	22	x, 11, 12, 14, 26, 44, 45, 46, 54, 55, 59, 60, 63, 66, 77, 80, 81, 89, 94, 100, 102, 104, 105, 106, 114, 116, 132, 137, 143, 149, 153, 156, 158, 160, 165, 176, 179, 185, 186
11	x		
11A	11, 34, 37, 77, 87, 110, 113, 114, 128, 183, 185		
11B	35, 63, 79, 102, 116		
11C	10, 14, 26, 36, 44, 88, 105, 153, 165, 179, 186	23	26, 46, 60, 62, 68, 100, 102, 116, 133
12	ix, 12, 37, 40, 48, 59, 89		
13	4, 6, 19, 39, 47, 67, 90, 126, 154, 158, 179	24	ix, 7, 31, 45, 59, 63, 73, 75, 80, 89, 100, 102, 109, 137, 140, 149
14	x	25	11, 64, 65, 83, 99, 153, 163
14A	12, 28, 40, 41, 42, 43, 66, 91, 97, 98, 106, 130, 156, 163, 173	26	6, 7, 11, 33, 64, 65, 83, 99, 108
14B	42, 43, 51, 79, 152, 154	27	x, 7, 14, 57, 60, 66, 91, 128, 129, 152, 153, 173, 180

227

Index of Ancient Sources

Gospel according to Thomas (cont.)

28	7, 11, 12, 39, 57, 62, 63, 67, 68, 70, 72, 76, 80, 82, 96, 100, 107, 114, 120, 126, 153, 158, 166, 176, 182, 186
29	7, 14, 16, 24, 67, 69, 82, 91, 107, 120, 127, 131, 136, 151, 182, 184, 186
30	7, 71, 116, 141
31	6, 7, 72
32	6, 7, 73, 74, 75, 76
33	x, 77
33A	7, 73, 74, 75, 84, 96, 107, 133, 161
33B	7, 63, 73, 75
34	9, 45, 72, 76
35	56, 73, 77, 132, 167
36	6, 7, 79, 130, 152, 167
37	ix, 7, 13, 19, 34, 55, 59, 80, 82, 89, 91, 105, 113, 117, 140, 147, 149, 151, 158, 177, 186
38	7, 82, 91, 159
39	x, 7
39A	6, 11, 12, 76, 83, 85, 86, 89, 99, 107, 154, 161, 171, 173
39B	84, 85, 86, 99
40	8, 11, 85, 86, 91, 99, 142
41	8, 70, 86, 115, 127
42	10, 11, 50, 87, 89, 152, 179
43	ix, 59, 89, 117, 158, 186
44	12, 82, 91
45	x
45A	43, 92, 110
45B	43, 92, 93
46	14, 25, 38, 44, 54, 55, 60, 77, 81, 94, 151
47	x, 95
47A	72, 95, 96, 97, 98, 133
47B	6, 95, 96, 97, 98
47C	95, 96, 97, 98
47D	95, 96, 97, 98
48	7, 26, 46, 51, 61, 99, 102, 132, 133, 146, 176
49	11, 12, 17, 26, 46, 49, 50, 62, 68, 77, 100, 102, 104, 109, 112, 137, 139, 146, 147, 151, 153, 165, 176, 179, 180, 183
50	11, 12, 13, 14, 17, 19, 23, 24, 39, 44, 50, 55, 62, 63, 81, 91, 94, 101, 102, 104, 114, 117, 122, 140, 149, 151, 152, 157, 165, 177, 183
51	ix, 11, 13, 14, 22, 56, 57, 59, 77, 89, 102, 104, 110, 114, 152, 157, 185
52	ix, 59, 63, 89, 105, 158
53	ix, 28, 41, 59, 82, 89, 91, 106, 130, 142, 156
54	14, 54, 60, 107, 112, 127, 142
55	7, 11, 41, 45, 95, 108, 118, 119, 133, 138, 151, 157, 168, 170, 175
56	7, 57, 109, 114, 118, 120, 122, 139, 145, 151, 182, 183
57	32, 54, 91, 110, 135, 165
58	25, 112
59	11, 13, 19, 82, 91, 105, 113, 140
60	x, 13, 35, 59, 86, 102, 114, 116, 126, 152, 180
61	x, 89
61A	89, 116, 152
61B	11, 17, 63, 89, 102, 116, 117, 133, 140, 149, 158, 159
62	x
62A	11, 29, 40, 47, 68, 74, 75, 84, 118, 149, 151, 159, 160, 180
62B	72, 119, 138
63	6, 7, 31, 32, 56, 110, 120, 127, 133, 135, 139, 165, 166, 182
64	x, 7, 32
64A	11, 56, 57, 121, 123, 125, 132, 138, 142, 146, 153, 163, 166, 172, 180, 182
64B	11, 56, 57, 91, 121, 123, 138, 142, 146, 163, 180, 182
65	ix, 7, 32, 124, 126, 138

Index of Ancient Sources

66	7, 126	88	8, 39, 83, 154
67	56, 107, 127, 140	89	28, 60, 156
68	112, 128, 129	90	11, 13, 102, 112, 114, 152, 157
69	x	91	ix, 6, 63, 80, 89, 117, 158, 166
69A	x, 6, 24, 91, 112, 129, 142	92	11, 82, 118, 157, 159, 162, 180
69B	x, 6, 12, 79, 107, 112, 130, 163, 169	93	x, 83, 161
70	24, 67, 70, 86, 127, 131, 165	94	27, 29, 47, 118, 157, 159, 162, 179, 180
71	132	95	7, 11, 163, 180
72	ix, 11, 59, 89, 126, 133, 143, 158	96	31, 32, 33, 54, 91, 110, 165, 166, 177
73	7, 31, 74, 110, 135, 136, 137, 138	97	7, 16, 32, 54, 56, 67, 70, 107, 110, 132, 166, 172, 177
74	ix, x, 7, 31, 56, 135, 136, 137, 138, 143, 158	98	7, 16, 17, 32, 54, 91, 110, 132, 142, 167, 177
75	x, 7, 11, 26, 31, 46, 55, 56, 60, 68, 100, 104, 135, 136, 137, 138, 143, 173	99	ix, 11, 54, 59, 60, 64, 83, 89, 91, 108, 143, 144, 168
76	x	100	x, 6, 89, 133, 157, 169
76A	31, 32, 54, 110, 119, 135, 136, 137, 138, 139, 167, 177	101	x, 7, 41, 45, 95, 108, 133, 142, 168, 170, 175
76B	120, 138, 139, 157, 180	102	6, 12, 76, 83, 89, 171, 184
77	x	103	56, 112, 172
77A	11, 19, 63, 102, 140, 141, 147, 149, 169	104	ix, 8, 11, 12, 41, 55, 66, 89, 137, 158, 173, 176, 186
77B	7, 11, 16, 19, 71, 141, 169	105	45, 108, 168, 170, 175
78	102, 126, 142, 146, 152, 153, 167, 180	106	7, 12, 13, 26, 51, 60, 68, 89, 99, 102, 105, 116, 133, 146, 151, 152, 153, 165, 176, 179, 186
79	ix, x	107	31, 32, 54, 137, 167, 177, 179
79A	59, 89, 91, 112, 137, 142, 143, 144, 158, 168	108	10, 11, 26, 27, 29, 39, 47, 60, 73, 77, 146, 149, 157, 159, 162, 165, 179
79B	112, 144	109	7, 32, 54, 138, 163, 166, 180, 182
80	7, 45, 57, 109, 114, 145, 151, 182, 183	110	13, 57, 109, 118, 120, 139, 142, 146, 180, 182
81	13, 166, 142, 146, 152, 153, 180, 182	111	7, 10, 19, 24, 34, 37, 38, 77, 91, 106, 109, 110, 113, 118, 131, 150, 151, 183, 185
82	1, 6, 14, 17, 33, 54, 82, 66, 147	112	6, 7, 70, 153, 185
83	11, 91, 102, 103, 148, 150	113	ix, 7, 11, 14, 22, 54, 59, 60, 72, 89, 91, 104, 110, 142
84	11, 16, 140, 148, 149, 150		
85	14, 53, 70, 94, 118, 146, 151, 152, 176		
86	6, 12, 13, 91, 151, 152, 153, 176, 180		
87	7, 8, 153, 184		

Index of Ancient Sources

114	ix, 11, 14, 16, 36, 44, 54, 55, 59, 60, 81, 82, 89, 91, 118, 133, 151, 176, 179, 185, 186

Gospel of Truth

18:11–21	100
21:18–25	100
21:25–30	100
31:35–32:34	178

Hypostasis of the Archons

87:11–88:24	103
87:11–20	69
88:1–15	69

Letter of Peter to Philip

136:5–15	60

On the Origin of the World

II,5,118:24—119:18	90

Paraphrase of Shem

2:14	117
3:22–26	117
9:17–19	117
10:16–17	117
39:24–29	117

Prayer of Thanksgiving

64:15–19	24

Sentences of Sextus

31:25–26	30

Teachings of Silvanus

84:15—85:21	129
85:1—86:23	77
87:27–30	30
93:28–30	23
95:7–11	84
105:26–34	30
107:17–25	30
116:19—117:5	22
116:27—117:5	23

Testimony of Truth

29:6–26	83
[30:16]	87

Book of Thomas the Contender

138:1–12	19
138:15–18	23

2 Treatise of the Great Seth

56:28	87
58:10	87

Tripartite Tractate

55:14—56:19	37
132:16–28	117

OTHER ANCIENT LITERATURE

Bala'izah

32:102	87
187:3	87

Kephalaia

120:31—121:2	109
163:27–29	27

Manichaean Psalms

154:1–12	137
257:20–22	30
263:17–19	137
263:29	137
264:13	137

www.ingramcontent.com/pod-product-compliance
Lightning Source LLC
Chambersburg PA
CBHW022336230426
43664CB00040B/1209